More G

Isle of Wight Ghosts
Book Two

Gay Baldwin

visit
www.ghost-island.com
for new stories

This book contains stories which originally appeared in
More Ghosts of the Isle of Wight

MORE GHOSTS

First published as
More Ghosts of the Isle of Wight
November 1992
Reprinted 1994

ISBN 0-9520062-0-0

Revised and republished
November 2007
as More Ghosts
Reprinted 2011

Published by Gay Baldwin
9 Pine Tree Close
Cowes
Isle of Wight
PO31 8DX
United Kingdom

Distributed by Gay Baldwin
Telephone: 01983 294651
E-mail: *gay@ghostisland.com*
www.ghostisland.com

Printed by Short Run Press, Exeter

ISBN 978-0-9520062-6-8

CHAPTERS

WHO BELIEVES IN GHOSTS?

*According to the dictionary, a ghost is: a spirit appearing after death, the soul,
a phantom, apparition, spectre, spook, visitant, revenant or wraith.*

When I decided to write this follow-up to the 'Original Ghosts of the
Isle of Wight', I was concerned that it might be difficult to find enough
stories to make the project worthwhile. I needn't have worried.
Accounts of new hauntings came flooding in. At one stage, I began to
think it was remarkable to find a house without a ghost of some sort!
In the thirty years since the first book was published, attitudes to ghosts
and the supernatural have undergone a considerable change. People of
all ages are interested in the subject and willing to keep an open mind
on something they don't understand.

Ghosts can, and do, appear almost anywhere. A house needn't be old
or historic to have one. Some very interesting hauntings have been
reported in a new housing estate in Wootton, while mischievous
poltergeists play tricks on the unwary in shops and cafes. Ghostly
soldiers haunt the Island's Victorian forts, while out at sea and on lonely
beaches, phantom ships still sail and ghosts of smugglers walk.

Some apparitions appear at set times each year, like the long-
vanished manor house of Knighton Gorges, which is said to materialise
on New Year's Eve; other ghosts come and go at random, sometimes
with years between sightings. A few hauntings consist of nothing more
than a sound; footsteps; ghostly music; the rustle of silk or sharp
knocking noises - the traditional 'things that go bump in the night.'

Some ghosts talk, whisper, shout and argue, seeming aware of their
surroundings, while others are oblivious to everything, following
centuries-old pathways through walls, walking above or below present-
day ground and floor levels.

Many families who live in a haunted house love the warm friendly
atmosphere that their ghost engenders. They like having it around, often
talking to it, giving it a name and treating it like a family pet.
Occasionally it really is, for in some homes the ghost of a favourite
animal lingers on.

Who can see ghosts? Almost anyone it seems. Even confirmed
sceptics have had their minds changed after witnessing the evidence
with their own eyes. People of all ages see, hear and smell ghosts.
Reliable, intelligent, credible professional people have come forward

with their stories. Many of them are puzzled and continue to be haunted by what they have seen and experienced. A few have turned to the Church for help and exorcisms have been performed with varying degrees of success.

Ghosts themselves come in all shapes and sizes. Some appear solid and real while others are wispy and ethereal. They have been described as a reflection in a plate glass window; while others are made up of dots or sparks of energy. In a few instances only part of the ghost has materialised, a disembodied hand or foot, head or torso.

In collecting these accounts, I have looked at the history behind a haunting. In many cases there is an obvious explanation; someone has been murdered, committed suicide or died a sudden and often violent death. Does tragedy, unhappiness or despair leave its imprint on a place? Can emotion linger in the atmosphere or in the fabric or a building like a psychic recording, to be replayed at intervals when the right atmosphere, or someone who is receptive and on the same wavelength, comes along? In other cases, I can find no apparent reason for a ghost's appearance. The spirit just doesn't want to move on. It is content to remain in its former home. The haunting is inexplicable.

I would like to thank everybody who has helped with my researches and those who have welcomed me into their homes and agreed to their names, addresses and stories being used. It cannot be easy to tell a complete stranger that you have a ghost. Special thanks to Steve Collins for the cover and to my long-suffering family who are now used to me calling out, 'That one's got a ghost!' whenever we go for a drive and spot a haunted house or place I have visited.

Check *www.ghostisland.com* for news, photographs and more new stories from the World's Most Haunted Island.

The Sun Inn and adjoining Read's Posting Establishment in Holyrood Street

The old Sun Inn at Newport, where a young French girl was murdered

Chapter One

GHOSTS OF NEWPORT

A DARK AND VIOLENT TRAGEDY

A bloodstained nightgown and a little leather shoe are the only evidence of a dark and violent tragedy that ended in a double murder more than two centuries ago. The scene of the crimes was the old Sun Inn at Holyrood Street, Newport, where for over two hundred years one of the innocent young victims has waited to tell her poignant story.

Half-forgotten rumours of the murders are still told by old Newport folk, but it was not until Graham Morris bought the former coaching inn after it closed in 1976, that he made a gruesome discovery in a tiny hidden attic room.

Graham, who later ran a shop dealing in antique militaria in part of the building, was renovating the old pub with his partner, builder Dave Knight, when he discovered the odd little room which had been boarded up and wallpapered over many years before. It had clearly lain empty and undisturbed for a very long time; for all it contained was a soldier's ancient pillbox hat.

However, hidden in a void behind the chimney, he came upon a dusty bundle of rags and a bag of ancient leather shoes. Inside the bundle was a very old white cotton nightgown, decorated with broderie anglais and heavily bloodstained. "It was covered in congealed blood which had gone brown with age and was absolutely macabre. It made me feel very uneasy. I burnt it in the back yard," Graham confessed.

In that same yard, he and Dave discovered an old well which also played a part in the tragedy. It contained at least 33 feet of water and although the well was pumped out by the Island's Fire Service, it was never excavated because the firemen deemed it too dangerous. The well has since been filled in.

The old pub was originally built in 1640 as a gentleman's residence. When it became a coaching inn is not clear, but it was certainly in use as early as 1730 as a busy staging post, with stabling in the nearby yard of what became Read's Posting Establishment.

Among the old shoes found by Graham was a small leather ankle boot, which was shown to a local nurse and medium Ivy Griffith. Ivy would often sit holding the little shoe to try to pick up some psychic clues from it. Over the next year, she and another medium were able to piece together the story of those tragic events at the Sun Inn, as the spirit of Francesca, a young French girl who had once owned the shoe and nightgown, relayed information to them.

Francesca's shoe was discovered at the old Sun Inn

"One day a very insistent little voice came through, asking, 'Parlez-vous Francais?' Every time we had a sitting, she was there again. She told us her name was Francesca and that she was fourteen years old."

Bit by bit the girl's pathetic story came out. It seemed she had been bought by the landlord of the inn for the sum of three crowns and put to work as a skivvy and serving wench. An orphan, born in France, she spoke little English and was very unhappy. A tiny slip of a girl, she had long, curly fair hair and large dark-lashed eyes.

Francesca had been kept busy running to and fro with tankards of ale until late into the night. She told Ivy how the customers would cheer the dog fighting and cock-fights that went on at the old inn.

Francesca fell in love with Ralph, a young stable lad at the Sun Inn, which was the staging post for coaches running between Cowes and Ryde. Ralph was kind to her and she started to blossom. Unfortunately, the little serving wench also caught the eye of the owner of a local print works, a man of standing and a pillar of the community. He watched and waited his chance. One night he found her alone in her attic room....

Although only fourteen, Francesca fell pregnant. But as her pregnancy advanced, she miscarried. As blood soaked her cotton nightgown, she lay close to death. The terrified girl whispered the name of her abuser and how he had forced himself upon her.

When word of this reached him, to prevent a scandal which would have ruined him in the town, he enlisted the help of friends who strangled the little French girl and dumped her body in the well. To cover their tracks and shift the blame, a scapegoat was found. Young

Ralph was the obvious choice. He, too, must die. Late one night, led by a local one-eyed ruffian known as the 'Pigman', a drunken rabble threw a rope over one of the wooden beams, stood the struggling young man on a crate, and kicked it from under him. They left him hanging there all night while they drank and caroused. Next morning Ralph was cut down and his body followed Francesca's into the well.

"Once she had told us the whole story, we never heard from Francesca again. She had wanted to have her case heard, as she put it, and for Ralph's name to be cleared. It took many months to piece all this together. You can't rush spirits," Ivy said knowingly.

Francesca and Ralph are together now, and have been for two centuries. "We are very happy now," she told Ivy. Apparently, her only regret is that she was not able to watch her child growing up. Ivy still has that little shoe, but any aura of sadness has been dispelled, purged and cleansed by Francesca herself.

(The earthbound spirits of Francesca, Ralph and their killers were laid to rest in 2001. Read their story in *Most Haunted Island*)

Horror in Holyrood Street

One day in their little shop which sells coins, antique militaria and medals, Graham Morris and Keith Shotter were startled when a customer told Graham, "There's a soldier in old-fashioned uniform standing right behind you. He says you have his medals in a drawer here." The woman described the ghost's uniform and told Graham his name and regiment.

Keith recalled, "When we searched the display drawers, there, on one of the shelves - which the customer couldn't see - was the ghostly soldier's medals. It gave us quite a jolt."

Above the shop however, things were not so peaceful. When their son and his girlfriend lived in one of the flats, Dave Knight and his wife Glenda were having a drink with some friends there one night. When Glenda told them the tale of the bloodstained nightgown, everyone just laughed. Suddenly, a picture 'jumped' off the wall and fell to the floor on the other side of the room. The string wasn't broken, and no one had been nearby when it fell. The room went very quiet. Suddenly Francesca's story did not seem so far-fetched after all.

It was in the attics here, some years earlier, that a poltergeist frightened the life out of Jean Sexton, her brother Trevor, and his wife. One night as they sat chatting in the kitchen of their flat at 11pm, a tremendous noise broke out in the empty attics above. The only access was a small wooden staircase between the kitchen and bedroom. Doors above them slammed incessantly, there was a heavy banging noise as if weighty furniture was being tossed about. On and on it went. They even barricaded the kitchen door to keep out whatever was up there.

When things eventually went quiet, they opened the door and peered up the little staircase. What they saw sent them slamming the kitchen door shut again. They watched the attic door slowly closing. Normally it did not close completely. Now it did. And then the lights dimmed…

Then came the strangest noise of that strange night. The sound a man might make grinding his boot heel into a scattering of gravel. They sat petrified, staring at the door, waiting for the handle to turn, while that thin, grating sound went on and on.

Finally, it ceased. "Everything's quiet," whispered Mrs Sexton. But she spoke too soon.

Suddenly from the attics came a thunderous noise, louder than anything they had yet heard. It shook the kitchen and set the stove vibrating. Not daring to move, they spent the rest of the night huddled in the kitchen until dawn. In the daylight they checked the attics. Nothing was out of place. However, behind the kitchen door was a small pile of gravel …

THE PHANTOM KING

Newport Grammar School, where King Charles I stayed

As one of Newport's oldest and most historic buildings, it is only fitting that the King James I Grammar School, which since 1618 has stood at the corner of Lower St James' Street and Lugley Street, is haunted.

King Charles I stayed there for sixty days in

Is this the ghost of King Charles I?

Autumn 1648, prior to signing the Treaty of Newport, using the large oak-panelled schoolroom as his presence chamber and sleeping in the room directly above. It was there, at dawn on November 30, that the king was seized by the Army and taken to Whitehall for his trial and subsequent execution.

This ghostly figure was caught on camera in the window behind Colin McMaster

In the centuries since, the school prospered, and many generations of Islanders were taught within its venerable old stone walls. It ceased to be a school in 1963, but five years later, youngsters' voices rang out once more when it became a youth centre. Some years ago, when Graham Dove was a youth leader there, he knew the old school had its ghosts. He both heard and felt them.

The supernatural activity seems to be centred around the first floor room above the headmaster's office, the one in which the unfortunate king slept. Footsteps are heard when the building is empty, echoing through deserted rooms. One youth leader who spent a night in that bedroom wouldn't go back. Although it had been midsummer, he said the room had gone icy cold and he had felt clammy and uncomfortable.

As youth centre members were intrigued by tales of ghouls and ghosts, Graham and the other leaders often organised 'Fright Nights' in the old school which were immensely scary - and popular. It was when they were clearing up after one such night in that bedroom that they, too, noticed a sudden drop in temperature. Something unseen walked through the room and out of the door. "We all felt it. There was something in there with us. The footsteps went right across the room and out onto the landing," Graham said. Whatever walks there enjoys company, for when the building was closed and locked, figures could be seen moving around a room lit by dim and flickering candles. It was that first floor bedroom again, of course.

One of the old school's ghosts was actually captured on film. A photograph of Colin McMaster taking part in karate championships held in the school grounds, shows a figure in a Cavalier's costume standing at the window behind (see page 11).

"I thought someone was having us on when I first saw these," Graham frowned. But then he realised that the window had been blocked by heavy weight training equipment. It was impossible for anyone to have been looking out of that room where King Charles spent his last days.

The Mauve Lady

Graham was certain that another of the school's ghosts was a woman. It was her footsteps he heard when the building was empty, and she has also been seen walking up and down Lugley Street. Affectionately known as the Mauve Lady of Lugley Street because of the mauve crinoline dress she wears, this gentle ghost haunts offices there.

In 1979, she was seen by two visiting Americans who were sheltering from a sudden thunderstorm in the doorway of the former Lamport Heyes and Co office, next door to the old school. Noticing a figure in a long cloak crossing the road towards them, they said, "What awful weather this is!" The woman said 'Aye' in apparent agreement and walked past them....straight *through* the solid wooden door.

Staff at the solicitors' office, which has now relocated, never saw her, but they occasionally heard her footsteps tap-tapping up the stairs, and searched for her in vain. "We became quite used to it after a while," said secretary, Margaret Snow.

Meanwhile, back at the youth centre, former caretaker Ray Edwards and his wife Joan became accustomed to the sweet smell of hay wafting down the staircase late at night after the youngsters had gone home.

In this building, now used as offices, the school's horses were once stabled, but not a wisp of hay has lain there for many years. However, on a warm, still evening, the old sweet aroma fills the air and sometimes, riding boots can be heard mounting those stairs....

GHOST WITH A SENSE OF FUN

Ghostly goings-on in council offices hit the headlines when women working in the former South Wight Borough Council's offices in Newport were so scared that they called the police.

While working overtime on the new electoral register, the six women all heard heavy footsteps in an empty office overhead; the sound of a chair being dragged across the floor; and a door opening. Margaret Chandler, who has now retired, said they had all been petrified.

"The police officer made a thorough search but didn't find anything. After he had gone, the noises started again, but we decided to stick it out. After that, we got quite used to strange things happening, and nicknamed our ghost 'Fred'.

"We never saw him, but we were convinced there was a ghost in the old building. He would sometimes take things such as scissors, pencils and other small objects, but would always bring them back again later. I am sure he had quite a sense of humour."

Heavy doors with spring closers would fly open, cupboard doors would also be opened and footsteps were heard in empty corridors. The

Chantry House is pictured here in the 1950s to the left of the Savoy cinema building

offices in Pyle Street incorporate Chantry House, which was originally one of Newport's religious foundations dating back to 1449. The present house was built in the mid-1720s.

Margaret worked at the Pyle Street offices, formerly the old Rural District Council headquarters, from 1966 until they closed in 1990. "I said when we moved out that poor old Fred would be lonely," she added. Margaret was often teased by colleagues who didn't believe in ghosts. However, she had the last laugh when a local postman confirmed her story. His mum had worked as cleaner there, but as she always refused to go into the building alone at night, he often had to accompany her. He agreed with Margaret, "This building is haunted!"

THE HAUNTING OF HAZARDS TERRACE

Hazards Terrace in Newport's ancient Sea Street was aptly named! For when the River Medina rose - and it frequently did - the little brick cottages there would flood. But for the Bloomfield family, who lived in number sixty-two, the name held a far more sinister significance.

Hazards Terrace in Sea Street was finally demolished in 1988 to make way for more car parking at County Hall. The haunted Number 62 can be seen on the left

From the time they moved there in 1947 until they left almost thirty years later, strange things would happen. Locked and fastened doors opened on their own, footsteps were heard crossing empty rooms, lamps were moved, and loud knocking and banging noises kept the children awake.

Brian Bloomfield, a former housing warden for Medina Borough Council in Ryde, was a boy of eight when he and his seven brothers and sisters moved into that house.

"Our mum just wouldn't believe there was anything going on there and refused to listen to us. But Dad knew differently, and he would be the one who came in with the torch in the middle of the night when we had heard or felt something."

In those days just after the war, there was no electricity and the family relied on oil lamps and candles for light, and coal fires for warmth. Brian recalled that the four-bedroom house always felt cold. "However close you sat to the fire, you never really got warm," he said with feeling.

Brian's most disturbing experience happened when an icy cold hand touched his forehead as he lay in bed one night. "I have never felt anything that cold before or since. As I lay there trembling with fright, 'something' shuffled out of the room and I heard it move slowly down the stairs and leave by the back door."

Brian's elder sister, Betty Beeney, also had unpleasant memories of that old house. She recalled that for many years, at 2.45am precisely each morning, there would be a creaking on the stairs, as if someone ... or something ... was climbing up towards the sleeping family.

Then one day it happened. Her bedroom door opened and she saw the outline of a man standing there. "I screamed for my dad, but by the time he came running in with his torch, the ghost was gone," she said.

Whatever haunted the old house also showed itself to young Brian, one morning just as dawn was breaking. The grey-white shape, which slowly took on a man's figure, was standing just by the door. As the terrified boy watched, it vanished into thin air. After Betty, too, experienced a touch from those freezing hands, she insisted on sleeping in the middle of the double bed - with her two sisters on the outside.

One night when a few of the children were alone in the house, they rushed in terror to their next door neighbour, Olive Hobbs, because 'something' had been banging so violently on an old tin bath hanging on a wall that it shook the whole house.

Olive must have sensed that something was 'not quite right' in the adjoining house for although she would drop in for a cuppa and a chat during the day, she would never set foot there after dark, recalled Betty.

An Unseen Presence

The old terrace was finally pulled down in 1988 to provide more parking space for County Hall. During the last years of its life, Hazards Terrace, which had become increasingly dilapidated, was temporary accommodation for the homeless.

At one time, the cottages were owned by Miss Gubbins who lived at nearby Hazards House (which was itself demolished to make way for the County Hall extension in the late 1960s). This, too, was haunted, and the housekeeper, Mrs Downer, often felt an unseen being pass her on the staircase in the 300-year-old house.

Len Knight is pictured amid the rubble of Number 62

During the 1930s, the Knight family, who left in 1938, occupied sixty-two Sea Street. However, Len Knight recalled nothing more alarming than lines of cockroaches migrating from the long-vanished Perkins bakery at the bottom of High Street. The family noticed no ghost during their time there, he said.

However, before the Bloomfields moved in, at least five people had passed away in number sixty-two.

Doris Hollowell, Len's older sister, said that their grandparents, a young brother and sister, and a subsequent tenant had all died in that house. Whose was the restless spirit responsible for haunting the Bloomfields? With the house now reduced to rubble, we shall never know.

Chapter Two

ISLAND ROADS ARE DIFFERENT

PHANTOM WITH NO FACE

Janet Eldridge made it a rule never to pick up hitchhikers. But one dark September night she foolishly broke that rule, with strange and terrifying consequences. As she drove across Staplers Heath towards Wootton, Janet was at peace with the world. The road ahead was empty; then her headlights picked out the figure of a woman trudging along the grass verge a hundred yards ahead.

Thinking the stranger's car must have broken down, she slowed down to offer her a lift for it was dark and they were in the middle of nowhere.

Janet stopped her van and waited. The woman who was wearing a long skirt and had a shawl tightly wrapped around her head and shoulders, leaned across the bonnet and peered inside. "I pushed my window back thinking she was coming round to the door to ask for a lift. But she just walked off across the road and straight *through* the hedge. She was a ghost and I had been about to offer her a lift," said Janet.

More horrifying still, as she sat trying to make sense of what she had seen, Janet realised the woman did not have a face. There was just a grey blankness where the features should have been. She started the van and took off home, breaking all the speed limits on the way.

Still in a state of shock, she told her husband Des what had happened, and as she re-lived her ordeal, found herself growing hotter and hotter. "I felt as if I was on fire. I was burning all over. I could almost feel the flames licking up over my arms. I could hear them crackle. The intense heat was agonising. I cried out to Des, 'I am burning. Please do something'. I was terrified. I thought I was going to burst into flames and become one of those cases of spontaneous combustion."

Janet's ordeal lasted several minutes and neither the cool night air nor cold wet flannels lessened the burning sensation. When it was finally over, Janet slept, mercifully without dreams.

It was more than two years before she could bring herself to drive along that stretch of road again on her own, and she still cannot pass the spot where the ghost disappeared, without a shudder.

"Who or what she was, I have no idea. She was obviously searching for something but she did not find it in my van. I sometimes wonder if perhaps she perished in a fire long ago and I caught an echo of this, somehow experiencing her last agonising moments as she burned."

COLLISION WITH A CAVALIER

One dark night as she drove towards Godshill, Pat Pledge saw a figure moving towards her car. She braked sharply, but not in time to avoid a collision. The friend who was with her screamed and Pat braced herself for the impact. None came.

As she drove straight through the man, he simply vanished leaving both women in shock. Pat can still recall every detail of that odd encounter because, as she soon realised, she had 'hit' a ghost.

"All I could see was the top of his tunic which was dark, with two rows of brass buttons down the front. He was wearing a black hat with a feather, and looked like a Civil War Cavalier. I stopped the car and sat there, trembling," Pat recalled.

Stranger still, it was on this very same stretch of road, just past Bohemia Corner, that she had seen a phantom horse floating just above the highway, some months earlier. Pat had slowed down so as not to frighten the animal, before noticing that its hooves did not touch the ground. As Pat watched, the grey horse drifted through a nearby hedge and vanished. "I am convinced there was some connection between the two apparitions and that they were probably horse and rider, but why I saw them several months apart, I will never know."

WRAITHS OF THE ROADS

In the village of Nettlestone, a ghostly woman in white is a well-known traffic hazard. Many motorists have rounded a corner by the village church only to find this apparition standing silently in the road.

Ted Jones was on his way home one night, with lads from his local darts team, when they literally ran into her. "We were in an old Buick and as we rounded the bend by the church, there she was. We all saw her but Ken Scriven who was at the wheel couldn't stop in time, and we went right *through* her."

They searched the road but could find no body, so they drove into Ryde to report the accident to the police. As the shaken young men stammered out their story, Police Constable Harry Coffin laughed. "We get quite a few reports of people knocking her down. Run along home, lads, you've just run over the White Lady of Nettlestone," he told them.

Another 'road ghost' has been seen at Vittlefields crossroads on the Forest Road, near Newport, where motorists have swerved to avoid a young motorcyclist who suddenly appeared in their path.

The shocked drivers were convinced the young man had been thrown from his machine and was lying badly injured, or dead, at the side of the road. They were right. He HAD been killed - many years earlier - during the last war, when, as a young dispatch rider, he collided with an army tank at that very spot.

GHOST TRAIN IN THE AIR

No train has run from Newport for almost half a century, so when Kay Liggens of Freshwater, caught a glimpse of an old locomotive with three carriages, steaming silently along, it had to be a ghost train she was seeing. Kay and her husband were walking down Holyrood Street one lunchtime, when she looked up and saw the apparition.

"I just stood there open-mouthed. I asked Roger when the last steam trains ran in Newport. 'Not since the 1960s,' he replied. It was then I knew for certain I had just seen a ghost train.

"It was only there for a few brief seconds and seemed to be crossing the brick viaduct, near the Newport to Cowes road. I heard nothing; the train was completely silent. It was just as though it was in mid-air. I saw the little old steam locomotive and two or three carriages but it was all so quick that I didn't take in any more detail."

It's likely the train Kay saw was travelling along the delightful, scenic line of the Newport Yarmouth Freshwater Railway, which opened in 1888, closing in 1953. Sadly, all traces of the little branch line have now vanished. In 1998, the old brick viaduct arches near St Cross Mill and the ramshackle shed, which served as the ticket office, were swept away. But that ghostly railway hasn't noticed, for it exists in a dark dimension of its own where steam trains run still. (Read more stories of ghost trains in *Even More Ghosts*)

GHOST TRAINS AT COWES

When you live in a house which backs onto a railway line you quickly get used to the noise of trains passing day and night, the sound of braking, shunting and whistles. However in 1986, when Margaret Eldridge moved into a semi-detached house in Gordon Road, Cowes, which has the former Cowes-Newport railway line at the bottom of the garden, she was astonished to hear the sound of the trains running through the old tunnel ... for the line had been abandoned many years earlier.

"I thought I was dreaming the first time it happened. There were the muffled sounds of a steam train and shunting noises coming from the back garden where the track used to run. I could never see anything, I would just hear them arriving at the station and pulling away again. There was the sound of wheels on the track, of engines and rolling stock being uncoupled, and the hiss of the steam engines. The train noises usually occurred very late at night or early in the morning when the town was quiet. My children never heard anything; they just laughed at me whenever I told them I had heard the sounds," Margaret said.

Judith Didham has heard those trains too. She has lived in the house since 1994 and occasionally, in the middle of the day, she, too hears those ghostly sounds as old-fashioned steam locomotives pass through the tunnel at the end of the garden. Bev Thomson knew nothing about the trains when she bought the house from Margaret, and although her room overlooks the garden and tunnel, she has yet to hear them. However, the affectionate little ghost of Whiskey the cat, who died in 2006, makes her presence felt regularly.

The spirit of an elderly man has been seen standing at the top of the stairs, and Judith is also aware of a former inhabitant of the house who passes through the hallway, leaving the faint but unmistakable aroma of cigarette smoke in his wake, as he checks that all is well.

THE MILLER'S GHOST

The ghostly, hunched figure of a miller at Yafford, near Shorwell, trudges across the road late at night, with a heavy sack on his back.

A mill has probably stood on the site since the Middle Ages. The present building dates back to the 1700s, and for over two centuries, its stones ground corn, barley and oats for local farmers. Until the mid 1960s, the mill was still paying its way, but when the last miller, 'Stocky' Salter, retired in 1970, the business closed for good.

John Attrill, who worked at Yafford Mill and lived in the old cottage next to the huge water wheel, often felt a strong, but friendly presence, around the house. The ghost also appeared near the old millpond, and when Yafford Mill was open to the public as a tourist attraction for a number of years, visitors saw him there too.

Two sightings several months apart, both happened at around 2am on clear moonlit nights. A taxi driver taking visitors to Brighstone Holiday Centre, saw a ghostly figure in front of him, crossing the lane outside the mill. The man who was carrying a heavy sack, simply vanished as he reached the mill.

Roger, John's son, also saw the same apparition, still with its sack, as he came home late one night. The description tallied in both cases, for Roger clearly saw a stooped figure with a weighty load on its shoulders traipsing across the lane to the mill... the ghostly miller on his way to grind a sack of corn perhaps?

THEY CARRIED SKULLS

It was a blustery, wet September night when Joan and Peter Gunston left the Ponda-Rosa at Ashey to drive back to Bembridge. As regular visitors to the Island, they had been out to a dinner-dance, and it was approaching midnight as they made their way home along back lanes, past Hardingshute and Nunwell.

Joan and Peter of Stevenage, who are both retired, saw no other traffic, but as they rounded a left-hand bend, there, clearly visible in the headlights, was a crowd of people dressed all in black. "There must have been fifty of them standing in the lane. They wore long, hooded robes and several were brandishing poles adorned with rams' skulls," said Joan.

Peter brought the car to a halt, telling his wife to lock her door and window. The figures started milling around the car, peering in at the frightened pair.

"They made no sound at all. Their faces were completely hidden by the hoods. Several of them raised their hands and one passed a finger across its throat in a threatening gesture. We were extremely scared by this time and Peter decided to drive on," Joan said.

"We thought they would get out of the way when the car started to move but they continued to encircle us. Peter put his foot down and I thought we would hit them. Instead the car passed right *through* the figures ... they weren't solid after all. As we made contact with them, they started to dissolve. After we had driven through the throng, I looked back. The lane was dark and completely empty."

Totally unnerved by their experience, Joan and Peter didn't stop to investigate further, but drove to Bembridge in a state of shock. They have never been down that lane since. "Who or what did we see that night? Could they have been the spirits of Satanists or perhaps witches from long ago?" wondered Joan.

The Gunstons' experience may indeed be associated with the occult. For almost 400 years ago, in the reign of Queen Elizabeth 1, witchcraft was practised in Ashey. It is recorded in the Ryde Court Rules, known as the Ashey Papers, that Agnes Porter, 'a widow residing within the jurisdiction of the Lord of the Manor of Ashey' was accused of being a witch was burnt at the stake. All her goods and chattels were forfeited.

Was what Joan and Peter witnessed that night a dark and sinister echo from the Island's pagan past? They believe it was.

THE PHANTOM MAID

When you don't believe in ghosts it can be difficult to admit you have actually seen one. Robin Thornton who owned and ran the Old Park Hotel at St Lawrence, near Ventnor, found himself in exactly that situation some years ago, when the phantom of a young Victorian maidservant floated past him.

There has been a dwelling on the site since the fourteenth century, although most of the building dates from the nineteenth century. Robin, who lived at Old Park for over 50 years, was working in the oldest part of the building when 'something' caught his eye.

Glancing up, he saw, with total disbelief, a young serving girl wearing a long black and white striped Victorian dress, with a lace cap over her black hair.

"It was quite fascinating and I was not at all afraid. She did not appear solid. It was just like looking at a reflection in a plate glass window. She seemed quite friendly and just moved past me and disappeared," he recalled.

Robin and his wife, Shirley, always found Old Park to be a warm and friendly place. A local psychic told them there was nothing evil there and certainly nothing to fear - but then, as Robin said, "Why should there be? There are no such things as ghosts!"

In 1999 the hotel was bought by the Sharp family, who run Old Park as a child-friendly holiday destination.

Chapter Three

HAUNTED FORTS AND MANORS

For centuries, the Island has been a strategic point for invading forces looking for a bridgehead into mainland Britain. A defence network still stands - from the Spithead forts in the eastern Solent to the Needles Battery, Golden Hill Fort and Fort Redoubt which guard the western approaches.

GHOSTS OF GOLDEN HILL

Ivor Allison and his wife, Jill, lived at Golden Hill Fort, Freshwater, after it was bought by Hayling Island businessman Wilfred Perkins in 1984. The fort was almost derelict when they arrived and the couple worked to build it into one of the Island's most unusual tourist attractions. They became familiar with its maze of winding corridors and arched rooms, often welcoming back ex-servicemen who were once stationed there. Ivor and Jill also came to know the fort ghosts. "One of them smokes a very sweet aromatic pipe and the aroma lingers in the corridor near our office in the early mornings or late at night when no visitors are around," Jill said.

"We often had people asking why there were servicemen in old-fashioned uniforms around the place. One lad saw a sailor leaning against a door in the room above the former Colonnade tea room, and this same figure was seen lounging in the doorway with his pipe."

Built between 1863 and 1872 at a cost of £38,000, the six-sided brick barracks, now a Grade 1 listed building, once housed 128 men and eight officers. Its guns were intended to cover the rear of the more vulnerable coastal batteries from attack by the French. Regiments whose men have been stationed at Golden Hill include the Royal Artillery, Duke of Cornwall's Light Infantry, the Isle of Wight Rifles, the Royal Hampshires and the Royal Militia of Jersey.

It is thought to be a sergeant-major from one of these regiments who fell, or was pushed, to his death during the First World War. Hated by his men, he plunged down one of the fort's two stone spiral staircases, breaking his neck. The 'accident' was hushed up; with official reports noting that he was 'killed in action'. His uniformed ghost has been seen on several occasions on the roof and in the old officers' mess.

A soldier fell to his death down these stairs

His fellow-phantom is a 19th century sailor, one of a small number of naval ratings stationed at Golden Hill. He, it is whispered, attempted to sell plans of the fort's defences to the French enemy. For his treason, he was condemned to death and spent his last lonely hours before execution in one of the fort's prison cells.

A local business woman who never believed in ghosts soon changed her mind when she moved to Golden Hill Fort to run the Colonnade Tea Rooms. Sheila Hughes would scoff at visitors who spoke of seeing the fort ghosts. To her it was all in the mind, or tales for tourists - until one midsummer day in 1988, when she, too, saw a ghost and became an instant, if reluctant, believer.

Sheila was in the back kitchen, once the fort's prison cells, where the double-barred windows and metal lined doors could be seen. "Everything was quiet and the first visitors had yet to arrive," she said. "Suddenly, I had a peculiar feeling that someone was standing in the kitchen with me. I went very cold and as I turned, I glimpsed the figure of a man standing beside me. I couldn't make out his features or what he was wearing. He disappeared as suddenly as he had come, leaving behind a feeling of chill and foreboding.

"I was icy cold, yet outside the sun was shining and it was a warm morning. I firmly believe there is a presence in that building and it is a very disturbed one. He transmitted a strong feeling of despair and fear."

Sheila was convinced Golden Hill Fort is not a lucky place. "Things go wrong there for no reason. It was folly to build it."

The Door Swung Open

In the early 1970s, Maureen Sutton of Freshwater worked at Golden Hill Fort for lampshade makers Readers Fancicraft. One night when she was there alone, finishing an order, she heard footsteps in the room with her. The unseen visitor came closer and closer.

"My nerve broke and I ran. I was in such a panic that I fell over and cut my head. With blood trickling down my face, I got out into the courtyard - and then I smelled pipe smoke in the cold evening air."

On another occasion, Maureen and several other girls took their coffee break outside on the verandah. As they sat chatting over steaming mugs, heavy steel bolts on the stairway door slid back by themselves and the door swung open. "The five of us jumped up, spilling hot coffee down our legs. Then we realised that whatever had opened the door, must have been on the verandah with us!

"Strange things would happen at the fort, but we all grew used to the ghosts. Articles in the workshop would disappear; whatever was haunting the fort had a streak of naughtiness. We would lift bags of fabric and find the bottoms ripped open. One day an old alarm clock which had no works inside, started to tick loudly," recalled Maureen.

In an engineering workshop below, which later became the Lord Palmerston pub, one of the workers often saw the ghost of the unfortunate sergeant-major, who would march in whenever he was working late. The man recognised the soldier's spirit and would pass the time of day with him. However, he refused to tell Maureen the ghost's name, because he said the dead officer's family still lived nearby in the West Wight.

Since being decommissioned, the fort enjoyed a chequered history as craft and Business Park, with a small museum and nightclub. Sadly, many initiatives there failed. Vandalism and fire accelerated the fort's decline and it was placed on the Buildings at Risk Register. In 2005, permission was granted to developers to convert the building into eighteen three and four-bedroom 'spectacular and individual luxury town houses'.

CONCERT FROM BEYOND THE GRAVE

A dozen regimental police are not easily frightened. But one night spent in the empty officers' quarters near Golden Hill Fort was more than they could stand. By 2am, they were so unnerved by their experiences in the old building that they took to their heels and ran.

Gerald Wildish, of Tennyson Road, Cowes, remembers it well. He was stationed at the fort for his National Service from 1959 to 1962 with the R.A.S.C., learning seamanship and boat handling. By then the fort's days were numbered, and Gerald's regiment, the last troops to be stationed on the Island, were preparing to move out. "It was a bleak, grim place," he recalled. "There were so few men left that twelve regimental police were brought in to do guard duties."

That cold, clear night in early spring, Gerald was standing his last night's guard duty. The reinforcements had arrived that afternoon, drawn their bedding, and were camping out in the empty officers' quarters across the road. At 11pm the huge fort gates were closed; Gerald and five other men settled down for their watch. At just after 2am came a tremendous disturbance. There was shouting, running footsteps and a hammering at the fort gates. All twelve regimental police, including a sergeant and four corporals, were outside the main gates in a state of undress, shouting to be let in. Gerald woke the duty cook, who brewed strong tea for the shaken men.

"They refused to go back to the officers' quarters that night and slept in the fort cells instead. They told us they had all heard classical piano music being played in the empty building. At first, they thought it was someone fooling around, but the music continued. They searched the place - but there wasn't a stick of furniture there, let alone a grand piano. Finally their nerve broke and they ran, wearing whatever uniform came to hand. We discovered later that the building may have been used in 1957 as a temporary mortuary for some of the dead from the Island's worst-ever air disaster," said Gerald.

This involved a Short Solent flying boat owned by Aquila Airways, which crashed shortly after take-off from Southampton, killing 45 people. It came down in a chalk pit at Shalcombe Farm and burst into flames. Two officers from Golden Hill Fort and a senior NCO were just yards away when the plane crashed; they led the rescue party dragging out dead and injured, until, with their own clothing alight, they were driven back. The passengers had been flying to Madeira via Lisbon, and

among the dead was a concert pianist on his way to an engagement. Did his spirit linger in the old deserted building until he could find an audience for his final concert from beyond the grave? Those twelve men certainly believed it did.

A flying boat crashed at Shalcombe in 1957

The old officers' quarters have been converted into flats, but the ghostly pianist has given no encore. Occasionally, the sound of footsteps is heard in an empty apartment, but they bother nobody. One resident wistfully wished the pianist would make a comeback. "Imagine having your very own concerts given by a ghost. I would love it," she sighed. (Read more stories of Golden Hill in *Even More Ghosts*)

THE HUNGRY GHOST

Over 100 years ago four soldiers died in an horrific explosion at Freshwater Redoubt, and at least one of them does not lie easy in his grave at the nearby churchyard. His ghost has been seen walking around the old garrison, searching it is said, for his dead comrades.

Perched on the cliff edge overlooking Freshwater Bay, the fort is privately owned by Chris and Kate Smith, who bought it in the year 2000. They plan to live there themselves and have been granted planning consent for apartments and a public function room at the fort.

The fort which had an upper and lower battery, barracks and parade ground, a deep dry moat and bridge, was constructed in 1856 to protect against attack by the French. But its guns which had a range of two miles, never fired in anger. The garrison could accommodate more than 30 men and officers, although in peacetime much smaller numbers were stationed there. During competitive artillery firing in front of senior officers on June 25th 1901, the breech block of the fort's right-hand 12-pounder gun blew out, killing Staff Gunnery Instructor Captain Arthur LeMesurier Bray, Gunner Charles Dorman, Gunner Rickets, and Bombardier Macdonald, also injuring six other men, including Colonel Nixon RA, Commander of the Isle of Wight Forces.

By 1918, the fort was disarmed. Ten years later, the War Office sold it to Amelia Bowland Cross for £600. In 1935, it was bought by Edward Henry Crinage, who added the top storey to create a family home. A tunnel for bathing access to Freshwater Bay was dug from an ammunition store in the Lower Battery.

During the Second World War, the fort was guarded, though not occupied, by the Home Guard. In 1970, American millionaire Byron DeWitt Daugherty bought the fort, but seldom visited it, selling it on instead to developer Mr Figgins. He built the tea-rooms in 1974 on the site of the old gun emplacements, and in 1977, sold the fort to Margit and Paddy Longmore.

Overlooking Freshwater Bay, Fort Redoubt was haunted by a hungry ghost

While they loved their unusual home, the couple were certain that ghosts still walked in the old fort. For two phantom soldiers were seen standing on a bridge over the deep dry moat surrounding the redoubt. One of them was smoking a cigarette. In the entrance tunnel lurked the dark shadow of another soldier. This man was said to have been crushed to death against the wall by a horse and cart. An eerie green light would flicker around the courtyard before disappearing into the former guardroom. Some old Freshwater fishermen told the Longmores that they avoided the fort after dark.

Margit and Paddy were certain their ghosts had a sense of humour and particular fondness for things electrical - especially video recorders, which often went haywire. Unable to sleep one night, Margit got up at 3am, made a coffee, and went back to bed. As she drifted off to sleep, she glanced at her radio alarm. The digital display showed 7am; so she got up, washed and dressed, ready to start the day.

"A ghost was having a joke at my expense because when I started work I found it was still the middle of the night. That electric clock had jumped forward four hours," she said.

In the tearooms, now, sadly, closed, a greedy ghost was heard smacking its lips over the choice of cakes. Margit explained, "Before the customers arrived one morning, my daughter and one of the waitresses were trying to decide which of the gateaux looked the most delicious. My daughter decided she liked the lemon cake the best."

"Mmmmmm", someone sighed with evident longing. Both girls spun around. But the room was empty. Whatever was in there with them had certainly sounded hungry….

THE LAUGHING CAVALIER

As one of the most ancient manor houses on the Island, Haseley just has to be haunted. With its rich and scandalous history, there should be ghosts aplenty. And the manor more than lives up to expectations.

Listed in the Domesday Book, Haseley is part Medieval, with various additions in Tudor, Stuart, Georgian and Victorian times. The monks of Quarr farmed Haseley for 400 years until the dissolution of the monasteries by King Henry VIII.

Its most colourful occupants were undoubtedly Dowsabelle Mill, a rich, beautiful widow and her lover, Sir Edward Horsey, the Captain of the Island. The pair threw riotous parties and entertained lavishly there, until Sir Edward's death, apparently of the plague, at Haseley in 1582.

The manor was sold to the Lord Chief Justice of England, Sir Thomas Fleming, one of the judges at the Gunpowder Plot trial, and it remained in the Fleming family for the next 350 years. In the 19th century, its fortunes began to decline when tenant farmers occupied it. In 1952, the house was sold and converted into farm workers' dwellings. By 1974, Haseley stood empty, semi-derelict and was almost beyond repair.

When Ray Young, a former Mayor of Brading, bought the manor with his late wife Krystyna in 1976, and opened it to the public, Haseley started to live again - as did its ghosts. One spirit, that of a handsome gentleman - Sir Edward Horsey perhaps - is always laughing. He has been seen on several occasions and one visitor, Charles Stewarts-Warwick, was able to sketch the laughing ghost. His drawing showed a figure in knickerbocker breeches, stockings, an open-necked shirt fastened near the waist with one button, a leather belt and boots and a wide-brimmed black hat. Charles thought the ghost was 'terribly jolly'.

"He threw back his head with silent laughter and I could actually see some of his blackened teeth," he said. Another visitor added to this description a few years later, when she, too, met the laughing ghost. "He had a beard, a moustache and wore a sword belt about his waist," said the startled woman.

One summer afternoon in 1991, several ladies praised the authenticity and attention to detail of Haseley's restoration. They were especially taken with the group of monks fishing in one of the old pools in the manor grounds. What they didn't realize, was that the monks were ghosts from a time when the manor belonged to Quarr Abbey, and the ponds, or stewes, were stocked with carp by the monks.

Some people felt an unhappy presence upstairs, which was probably Haseley's tragic young ghost, Amelia Bastiani, who hanged herself in an attic room on May 7th 1854. The inquest, held the next day, heard how another serving maid discovered her body. She was buried immediately after the inquest in an unmarked grave, in unconsecrated ground.

Hers was a sad little story. A local beauty, Amelia fell in love with a charming visitor to Haseley, a London surgeon who 'took advantage' of her. By the time Amelia discovered she was with child, her former lover was engaged to marry a daughter of the manor. The wedding was to take place the very next day.

Distraught, disgraced and pregnant, poor Amelia told fellow servants, "This is my last day's work at Haseley." Then she went, alone, to her attic room to commit suicide. Her former lover continued with his wedding on the day that Amelia was buried. Self-destruction was a mortal sin, and an echo of Amelia's despair lingers in those attic rooms.

Another melancholy spirit at the manor is thought to be an 18th century daughter of the Fleming family.

This girl too, loved unwisely with unhappy consequences, falling in love with a man who was socially her inferior. Her father forbade the match, but they took no notice. When he discovered her disobedience, Squire Fleming whipped his daughter so savagely that she was scarred for life.

For the rest of her life she wore long-sleeved dresses to hide the livid marks on her arms and body. The beating also left her mentally scarred. She died, a bitter and lonely spinster. Her spirit has not found peace and Angie Newnham, a psychic, saw her mournful ghost when she worked at Haseley in the 1980s.

"I was working in the house when I felt drawn to the window overlooking the gardens near the stream. Looking out, I saw the ghost of a lady aged about thirty, walking in the sunshine. She wore a turquoise day-dress with a bustle. Her long-sleeved dress had fancy pointed cuffs that completely hid her arms and hands. She wore her light brown hair piled up under a bonnet," added Angie.

Haunted Haseley Manor is pictured here in 1992, when it was open to the public

James, Ray Young's son, was born at Haseley, and as a toddler, he loved to explore the old house. "When we were dismantling a concrete wall dividing the house, we lost James one day. We eventually found him wandering about in the empty main house. He wasn't frightened and told us he had been talking to 'the lady', Ray said."

The Friendly Ghost

As a boy of four, Freddie Morris moved with his family to Haseley when his father worked on the farm there. At that time, the manor house was divided into two houses. "We had the right-hand half which included the great kitchen. My mother was aware that from a young age I could see and hear spirits - my grandmother had been psychic too. One night I slept in the main bedroom, below what we knew as the 'tack room'. I think I had been moved there because I had measles or chickenpox and it was nearer mum's room. My sister, who normally had that room, had been moved for the duration of my illness. Everything was OK when my mother put me to bed, but in the middle of the night, I was aware of the bed lifting and turning around on its axis. I was so scared that I pulled the blankets over my head. The next morning, when she found my bed had been turned around, my mother accused me and my sister of playing games - but she knew that something 'odd' had happened, because she moved me to another bedroom.

"When I visited the manor during Ray Young's tenure, I saw that the floor and ceiling between the tack room and bedroom had been removed (possibly due to rot as there was a large hole in the ceiling and roof when we lived there). This bedroom was the one where Mr Young had the tableau of Sir Edward Horsey dying of plague in his bed.

"I recall there were old medlar and walnut trees in the garden, where I used to sit with my 'friend' Mr Downer (who no one else could see). Mr Downer was a kindly spirit, but he had a mischievous sense of humour, for he would tell me to do things, which got me into trouble. "Sometimes he would meet me by the gate which led from the garden into the farmyard, but usually he was by the main gate to the drive. He had grey hair, a bushy beard and wore a long leather apron. He told me he was 'the ostler', but I didn't know what this was. Years later when I saw a picture of someone in a similar apron, I realised that Mr Downer had worked with horses.

"On one occasion, mum was burning some household rubbish, including some curtains, which 'Mr Downer' told me to pick up. I did so and promptly dropped the cloth again as it was red hot. I bore the scar on my fingers for many years!

"I remember there was a water tank by the back door. I was afraid of heights, but my sister Jacqueline would climb up and look in. I remember a seeing a ghostly lady in a long dress with an apron and bonnet nearby. She gave my sister a 'helping shove' and pushed her in. I got the blame!"

Sharon Fox of Sandown was just 18 when she worked in the tea-rooms and house at Haseley. She would often hear the sound of small feet walking across the floor in the tea-rooms and look over the counter, expecting to see one of the owners' dogs; but there was nothing there. Upstairs in the main bedroom however, and in a little staircase off it, there was a far more uncomfortable feeling.

"Sometimes as I crossed the room, the hairs on the back of my neck would go up, the temperature would fall and become freezing cold. I would feel a confusion of emotions there with anger, sadness, vindictiveness, despair and guilt. Strangely, I could actually step in and out of this concentration of feelings, it was very localised. After a few days, I had had enough. I ran downstairs and said to Krystyna Young, 'I don't mind the ghost in the tea-room but I can't stand the one upstairs.' When she told me that was where the serving maid had hung herself, I was shocked, because I hadn't heard that story. Suddenly, that whirl of emotions made sense."

In the year 2000, Ray sold Haseley Manor to Anthony and Vivienne Roberts, both of whom are doctors. They have continued the renovation and improvement works started by Ray, and although it is no longer open to the public, Haseley enjoyed a brief spell as a popular wedding venue for several years.

Anthony is sceptical of Haseley's haunted past, but Vivienne keeps a more open mind, particularly since she has heard the sound of ghostly footsteps when she has been alone there at night.

These ghosts from the manor's chequered past never bothered Ray. They moved about the manor on their ghostly business keeping themselves very much to themselves. Many manors have ghosts and it is only fitting that such a fine old house as Haseley should have its share.

SOBBING IN THE ATTIC

When the Pinder family bought Pidford Manor, they didn't realise that, along with one of the Island's most historic and charming houses, they would also be taking on the resident ghosts.

Although it is considered one of the Island's minor manors, there has been a house at Pidford since 1301. Sir James Worsley, a page to King Henry VII, occupied a subsequent manor house and in 1840, the rebuilt Pidford Manor became the residence of authoress Elizabeth Sewell, who wrote many of her 57 books there.

Sheila Pinder was alone in the house one night when she heard loud and angry crying coming from one of the old attic nurseries. It was so real that she raced upstairs. But as she reached the landing, the noise stopped abruptly.

"It was definitely a child sobbing uncontrollably in a hurt and angry way. It made me very uneasy," Sheila admitted. Later, she heard from the manor's previous owners, Dr and Mrs Denman Johnson who lived at Pidford for eleven years, that the ghost of a child had been seen and heard in the same part of the house.

Mrs Denman Johnson often sensed a young child standing by her bed in the night. Once, the feeling was so strong that she hurried upstairs to the attic bedrooms to check on her own sleeping daughters. Climbing the stairs, she saw a small child's hand going up the staircase too. Only the hand was visible, and it was at the 'wrong' level. The family learned later that the old attic stairs had been moved from their original position.

"I never saw anything else," said the former lady of the manor. "I felt it was a young girl and she was unhappy. My children would sometimes hear footsteps and creaking of floorboards on the landing between their attic rooms, but after we had been there a while, the feeling disappeared. The house was full of children and laughter so I don't think the little ghost was lonely any longer."

Pidford's other ghost is a corpulent elderly gentleman in his night attire. Sheila Pinder saw him standing in front of her bedroom window early one morning. He wore an oriental brocade dressing-gown, patterned in rich dark colours of crimson and gold, and on his head was an odd little nightcap. "He seemed to be looking straight at me and I was really quite frightened. I decided to leave him to it and went downstairs to make a cup of coffee. When I returned, the bedroom was empty."

Shortly after moving in, Sheila invited her local priest to bless the house. "He asked me if I had seen any ghosts there. I thought this was rather a strange question for a priest. Now I know why," she said.

A HANDFUL OF TINY BONES

A baby's crying so distressed the nanny at a Seaview home that she left her job. Nothing she did could comfort the infant, for it was a ghost.

Although this happened many years ago, Ted Jones, of Ryde, was haunted by the pathetic little tale. He was just a lad of 16 when it happened, working as a painter with a local firm, renovating a large, eighteenth century house in Oakhill Road.

The nanny had left, it was said, distressed because of the ghostly crying and the sound of running water, which were always heard together. A local clergyman was asked to bless the house to rid it of the unwanted presence.

It didn't work. The crying continued until a plumber came to check and renew the pipes. Up in the roof, directly over the room where the sounds were heard, he found an ancient lead-lined water tank. It was bone dry; full of the dust and debris of many years. It also contained some fragile bleached white bones. A tiny baby's bones. The tank was removed, and from that day onwards the crying stopped. It was never heard again.

Chapter Four

ADVENTURES IN TIME

THE PUB THAT VANISHED

One dark November night, Laurie West set out from Newtown with a friend, for what turned out to be the strangest night of their lives. On that cold, wet evening in 1982, they came upon a pub that doesn't exist and shared a drink with some very unsociable spirits.

Laurie lives and works at Ryde. He is still puzzled by his experiences that night, which, years later, remain etched in his memory. He has made every effort to find that old pub again and spent many hours driving the lanes around Calbourne trying to locate it. He undertook historical research in the Island's archives in an effort to trace it, and questioned local people as to its whereabouts. But Laurie reached the inescapable conclusion that he was drinking in a ghost-pub.

The pub was called 'The Vulcan' or 'The Falcon'. "I don't remember which; it did not seem significant at the time," said Laurie. "I picked up my friend at Newtown and we set out to have a drink. As we drove towards Shalfleet, I noticed a lane on our left and asked my companion if he had ever been along it.

"I thought later it was odd that my friend did not recognise the turning, because he had lived in the Newtown area for many years. Some way down the lane, we saw a pub on the right and pulled onto the empty gravelled area at the front. The pub signboard was swinging and creaking in the wind, high above the door.

"We entered through a small porch and went into the lounge bar first. This was full of brown, heavy leather furniture, and was deserted. It had an unpleasant chilly feeling, so we made for the public bar instead."

Laurie recalls that this bar had a flagstone floor, a large, empty and cold fireplace, old wooden tables and chairs. The atmosphere was cheerless and unfriendly.

A shabbily-dressed woman was serving behind the bar, and there were about fifteen other people in the room, all middle-aged or older, wearing drab old-fashioned clothes.

"Everybody stopped talking and stared as we came in. It was quite unnerving. All eyes were upon us. They continued to watch as we got our drinks. I foolishly asked for a gin and ginger beer - a few days earlier somebody had suggested I should try it. The barmaid said, 'We don't have that.' So I said I would have gin and ginger ale instead. It was horrible! We sat down at one of the tables. The people around us resumed their conversations, but kept glancing at us. We were not at all welcome. We felt like intruders."

Laurie recalls paying for the drinks with a pound note and being given the change in florin and shilling coins, which did not strike him as unusual, since they doubled as 10p and 5p pieces in decimal coinage.

With no fire in the large fireplace, the bar felt cold. The two men sipped their drinks, feeling more and more uncomfortable. "We certainly didn't want another, so we left. I couldn't wait to get out of the place. Every pair of eyes in the room followed our departure."

They hurried out into the cold clear night with a feeling of great relief. Their car was still the only vehicle in the deserted car park. As they drove off down the lane, Laurie could see the pub sign still swinging and creaking in the wind.

"A short way down the road, we were astonished to find ourselves at the Sun Inn at Calbourne. It just wasn't possible. We had not crossed the main Newport-Yarmouth road at any point. I thought at the time it was strange that the two pubs should have been so close together."

The two men had one drink there - in normal cheerful surroundings - then Laurie took his friend back at Newtown and drove home to Ryde, still puzzling about that inhospitable pub. The experience so disturbed him that a few days later he went back in daylight, determined to visit the pub again and find out why it was so unfriendly.

However …"I never found the pub again. I drove all over the place trying to retrace our route. That lane just wasn't there any more. Finally, I went into the Sun Inn in Calbourne and asked if there was another pub nearby. There wasn't. But I already knew that!" *(Is it significant that the original Sun Inn was totally destroyed by fire in April 1894?)*

When Laurie inquired at the County Archives about old pubs in the area, he drew another blank. After hearing his story, the archivist told Laurie he must have had a 'few too many' that night, because there was no such place. So the mystery remains. Both Laurie and his friend were at the pub that night. They sensed at the time that something was very wrong. Now they know why. The Vulcan or Falcon just doesn't exist. Not in this world or dimension, anyway....

(Read of another vanishing pub near Brighstone in *Most Haunted Island*)

TRAVELLER IN TIME

A Victorian house in Wootton still haunts the dreams of electrical engineer Dan Cox, for it was there, in the early 1970s, that he went back in time and glimpsed his home as it was in the 1920s.

It was an incredible and terrifying experience for Dan, who, even now, is unable to explain or understand it, although he can recall details of that winter's night with startling clarity. "It was no dream, that I do know, but whether I slipped back in time or saw some kind of ghost house, I will never be sure."

In 1968, Dan, then aged twenty, moved with his parents and younger brother George, to an unfurnished flat in The Brannons, a large Victorian house in Station Road. The family had a spacious apartment on the ground floor. The rooms were grand, with high ceilings, and what was once the lounge or withdrawing room was divided into two bedrooms. Dan and George shared one; their parents had the adjoining room.

One bright moonlit night, Dan awoke at 2am with an overwhelming feeling that something was dreadfully wrong. Glancing over at George's bed, he saw a large, grey upholstered sofa instead!

Thinking he must still be dreaming, Dan turned over in bed only to find the partition wall had gone. In place of his parents' bed, he saw the glowing embers of a dying fire in an old-fashioned cast-iron grate. "I was wide awake by this time," said Dan. "At first I was puzzled, but as the seconds ticked by, I began to panic. This was the room as it would have been 50 years earlier. My parents and brother had disappeared. Where on earth was I?"

Dan was no longer conscious of his own body and could not see his bed. "I felt no sensation. There was no sound; the room felt neither cold nor warm. I could see a clock on the mantelpiece, but it made no sound. The fire emitted no heat; there was no crackle of burning coals."

Looking desperately around the strange room, Dan noticed that the walls were covered with leafy patterned wallpaper. He saw too, that electricity had been newly installed in the house for a glass lampshade hung in the centre of the room and a cable had been fixed on top of the wallpaper. "Working with electrics, I notice these things," Dan explained. He also remembers seeing a large piece of furniture - a piano or bureau - against a wall. As the seconds passed and the room did not waver or change back, Dan wondered if he should get up and explore the rest of the house.

But he reasoned, "I could not bring myself to get out of bed. I froze at the thought I might never find the bed again and be somehow trapped there in a time before I was born."

Dan closed his eyes tightly and concentrated on feeling his body again, then moved back into his original position. When he opened his eyes, to his great relief, his brother George was there once more, in place of the sofa. The room had returned to normal.

Dan believes that for those few minutes he somehow slipped or drifted 'back' in time. This has never happened to him again. But even today, if he wakes in the middle of the night, he always opens his eyes very, very warily...

THE BLOODSTAINED FOOTPRINTS

The Mystery of the Bloodstained Footprints and The Shadow at the Window sound like great titles for plays. But at the Trinity Theatre, Cowes, if the actors aren't careful they find their theatre ghost literally getting in on the act and trying to steal the show.

The 199-seat theatre, just off Bath Road, is the permanent home of the Cowes Amateur Operatic and Dramatic Society (known locally as CAODS) who are quite used to the pranks of their ghost. It is company policy that all the props must be checked before every performance, for they have a nasty habit of disappearing or being moved about the stage.

The ghost is such an accepted part of the company that it has even featured in Stage Whisper, the CAODS monthly magazine, in a series of cartoons, with each one starting: 'Trinity Spook Says...'

Chris Buckett joined the company in 1975, and was formerly Theatre Club manager, also doubling as theatre technician and a stage manager. He heard and glimpsed the theatre ghost on several occasions.

Supernatural activity in the theatre seems to be centred around a storage room in the north-west corner of the building, and in the lighting box above. When Chris first saw the ghost, it was standing in the doorway to that room one summer evening, dressed all in black. He shouted, "Can I help you?" The figure vanished. Since then it has been seen by other members of the company, always in the same doorway.

That room is always cold, an unnatural cold some say, even in midsummer when the rest of the theatre is hot and airless. Leading up to the lighting box is a wooden ladder, which Chris would never go up if he was alone in the theatre. He admitted he felt afraid there.

Even when that tiny room is locked and empty, figures have been seen moving between windows, which resemble eyes high up in the wall. People in the theatre often find their gaze being drawn there.

When a cast-iron fireplace was needed as a prop,

A ghost treads the boards at Trinity Theatre in Cowes

Chris's brother, Michael, and three friends volunteered to collect it. All four men struggled to lift the heavy fireplace onto the stage, but when they turned away to build the rest of the set, that fireplace 'jumped' off the stage, landed several yards away in the auditorium and shattered.

Then there is the mystery of the footprints, which come and go for no apparent reason. They were first noticed when the wooden floor was scrubbed clean after the theatre had been used as a nightclub as part of the town's annual Cowes Week festivities. Before the seats could be replaced, the huge, dark footprints faded away then reappeared, weaving their way across the wooden boards. Some days they are visible, at other times there is nothing to be seen.

A psychic who investigated the old theatre, declared that the footprints, which lead from the back storeroom, were made by blood which had soaked into the floor. When he attempted to stand on a pair of the prints, he was knocked to the ground by some unseen but very powerful force. He said that during the last war, a man who died in the building when it was used as a Red Cross and WRVS station for people injured in the Blitz, had made them.

During the war, Trinity Hall was used for military purposes, including troop concerts given by Wrens from the nearby HMS Vectis, which was situated in Osborne Court. One Wren with a beautiful soprano voice was in mid-song when the air raid sirens sounded. The concert halted as everyone made their way to the shelters. She however, never made it to safety and was killed. Her song remained unfinished.

The Wren's spirit is said to haunt the auditorium as she waits to resume her number, and curiously, a butterfly appears in the theatre at least once during every show. Regardless of the time of year, it hovers around the spotlights and sometimes alights on members of the cast. It is seen by players and audience alike, and is regarded as a lucky omen by all who play on stage at Trinity Theatre.

Impossible Footsteps

Trinity Hall was built in 1914 as a hall for Holy Trinity Church. It occupies the site of The Grove, a large house built in 1833 for Mrs Sarah Goodwin who financed the building of Holy Trinity Church.

Footsteps are sometimes heard in the empty theatre, moving down the centre of the auditorium both to and from the stage. Members of CAODS have heard them, but only when there are few people about. Curiously for a theatre ghost, this one seems shy of appearing before an audience.

It is thought that those footsteps may belong to a ghostly guest artiste who treads the boards at Trinity because his own theatre has disappeared. Albert DuBois recited comic monologues at the old Shanklin Pier Theatre in the 1890s but passed away after only his second season there. In the century since, however, he has made several come-backs. Performers in the old theatre heard his footsteps, always seven of them, coming up onto the stage. There were even plans to issue the ghost with his own Equity card!

When the old pier theatre closed in 1979,

Dark blood-stained footprints sometimes appear

those plush red velvet seats (and the resident ghost) went to the Trinity Theatre, where now it appears that Albert's ghost continues to tread the boards.

'MESSY LITTLE POLTERGEIST'

Next to the Trinity Theatre, in the Beken & Son photographic shop, 'George' the poltergeist once made mischief. Although a vicar from Holy Trinity Church exorcised the old shop in Bath Road in 1960, it was clearly not successful.

Whether a link exists between the theatre ghosts and George, no one knows. Ros Booker, who ran the shop for more than thirty years, was accustomed to George and his antics, and she became quite concerned if she did not hear from him for a while.

Handbags and camera bags were his speciality. He loved to throw them about the shop if they were left on a particular shelf. Many years ago, when a Miss Burland, who sold fashion goods and yachting accessories, ran the premises she would often complain that the poltergeist, which she described as a 'nasty, naughty little thing', had left dirt and mess there during the night. Displays of handbags were sent flying so often, that eventually in 1960, the local minister was summoned to cleanse the shop of its unwanted spirit.

George, however, refused to budge and when Bekens took over the premises, filling them with film and camera equipment, he happily switched his attentions to the camera bags stacked on shelves overhead. "I often came in to find bags on the floor, and when I was serving, the odd bag would often be thrown right across the shop," said Ros.

The same psychic who investigated the nearby theatre was also interested in George's activities. Was he the ghost of a mail-coach driver throwing bags out as he passed staging posts, such as the one at the gates to The Grove where the shop now stands?

Ros was sure he was perfectly harmless and enjoyed having him around. "I sometimes had to tell him off when he started throwing things but otherwise, I always felt he was a happy little soul and I didn't mind his antics at all."

Ros has now retired and the business has changed hands. Owner, Rod Hillier, reports that ghostly activity in the shop has ceased.

The outline of a severed hand and the name William Fleming are carved into old oak beams at Rose Cottage in Roud, where a ghostly hand was seen in 1976

Chapter Five

GHOSTS WITH REGULAR HABITS

Some ghosts are creatures of habit and are only seen at a certain time; on particular days, dates; or at certain times of the year...

ONLY ON A FRIDAY

The outline of a severed hand and the word 'Friday' carved into an oak beam at an old cottage near Godshill, were treated as mere amusing curiosities by new owners when they moved in. They should have known better ....

Rose Cottage, in Roud, has a tranquil and welcoming atmosphere. A delightful place, built from old grey stone in the early 1700s, it stands on the site of a much earlier dwelling which was once in tithe to nearby Great Appleford.

When Peter and Ann Moreton moved to Rose Cottage in 1976, with daughters Charlotte and Elizabeth, they loved their new home and delighted in showing visitors that odd carving on a beam above the fireplace. A man's huge left hand with fingers splayed had been traced and carved there, together with the name *'William Fleming'* and the date, *FRIDAY 22nd March 1774*. The words *"He that hath given to the poor leadeth to the LORD"* are also carved into the beam.

Shortly after moving in, Peter and Ann noticed something was wrong at Rose Cottage. As they sat chatting with friends in front of the log fire, everyone suddenly stopped talking and listened. For in the room with them was the sound of water being poured from a jug onto the floor.

Strange things always happened on Fridays. The whole cottage would fill with a feeling of foreboding. Lights flickered and went out; the power failed; bathroom taps were turned full on by an unseen hand. Things became so bad, that on Fridays, Ann refused to stay in the cottage and took the children to her in-laws until Peter came home from work.

The little girls spoke of seeing bright lights and a ghostly figure in their bedrooms. Charlotte also saw a ghost-girl aged about ten, with long blonde hair, standing in her parents' room one day. Their dog would sit at the top of the staircase watching something invisible to a human eye as it passed by on the stairs, and Peter's brother-in-law,

Graham, also found his attention drawn to the same spot when he came to stay. He often slept downstairs on the settee at Rose Cottage, but never spoke of what he had seen, in case it worried the family. However, one night, he rang Peter to say he had just attended a séance. Never having been to one before, Graham had been a little surprised when a voice claiming to be that of a 'Brother John' had tried to contact him.

This spirit claimed to be the ghostly monk who walked up and down the staircase at Rose Cottage when Graham was staying there. Brother John also told him the cottage had once been called Rose Hill, and that he had worked as a stonemason there almost 600 years ago. But Brother John did not mention the carved hand, and Fridays continued to be bad days and Ann dreaded them. An almost tangible, unpleasant feeling pervaded the cottage but only on a Friday. Then she discovered why...

The Hand in the Mirror

"I was sitting at the mirror putting on my make-up, when I saw a hand behind me. It was a large, fleshy man's hand, which had been severed at the wrist; the edges were jagged and bloody," Ann said.

"I literally froze. I was petrified. Then something in me said, 'enough is enough'. I lost control and swore at the awful apparition. I told it in no uncertain terms to 'go away', then I closed my eyes. When I opened them again, the hand was still there. Suddenly it vanished with a 'wooshing' noise and somehow I knew that it wasn't coming back."

Since then, Fridays haven't been a problem. The cottage feels at peace and if Brother John still wanders up and down the stairs, he bothers no one. Peter and Ann occasionally notice the smell of aromatic tobacco coming from a corner of the lounge by the settee. Perhaps old William Fleming is enjoying a quiet pipe of baccy at the end of the day.

THE PHANTOM FARRIER

A phantom farrier continued to work at his anvil forging iron shoes for ghostly horses at a lonely Brighstone farm. Sounds of hammering and the ring of metal on metal could be heard, along with the snorting and stamping of the animals waiting to be shod.

Chilton Farm, which stands just off the Military Road, is recorded in the Domesday Book. The present farmhouse was built in the early 1600s after an earlier house burnt down. Since 1971, it has been the home of farmers Sue and Richard Fisk, and their family.

The house itself was haunted by the sad little shade of a young girl who lived her short life there and died at the age of twelve, over a century ago. "We never knew her name, we would just hear her weeping. The sound always seemed to come from one of the bedrooms, but whenever we went upstairs to look, it would stop," said Sue.

There was often a strong feeling of sadness in the far sitting-room where the girl's weeping originated. Cilla Worsfold, Sue's younger sister, also heard that crying - a sound she could not forget. Perhaps the ghostly child cried because she was lonely, for nothing has been heard from her since Jeremy and Victoria, Sue's children, were born.

Outside in barns and stables, which were converted into holiday cottages, things were not so peaceful. Guests staying in one particular cottage complained of being woken by a loud banging and hammering, which seemed to come from inside one of the old stone walls.

One woman told Sue she had actually seen the ghost of a farrier at work with hammer and anvil making the horseshoes in a corner of the bedroom. A couple of months later, two more guests mentioned they had been kept awake by loud noises coming from a corner of the bedroom. This happened two nights running, although strangely, no one in the adjoining cottages heard a sound.

The following autumn, two girls holidaying in the same cottage checked out a day early. They had enjoyed their stay, they said - apart from the noises. The girls explained that two nights running, they were woken by banging, hammering and the sound of animals moving around. The noises came from the empty cottage next door.

Today, all is quiet at Chilton Farm. The ghostly farrier has downed tools and disappeared. Why he only worked on Friday and Saturday nights remains a mystery. Sue added, "We never discovered why he was only heard on those nights, or why people sleeping in adjoining cottages were never disturbed. It really was strange."

SPIRIT ON VACATION

For more than fifty years, the ghost of an aviator dropped in at the Brading guest-house where he had spent many happy holidays. Each September the long-dead pilot appeared in his old room, much to the surprise of the current guests; there he would stay for exactly a month.

Graham Redfern who ran the 17th century guest-house at Morton Farm with his wife Pat, is the fifth generation of his family to live there.

He can recall the annual arrival of the ghost-pilot, and also remembers how the phantom who had outstayed his welcome, was sent packing by the Bishop of Portsmouth in 1958.

The Bishop was summoned by Graham's exasperated mother who was tired of the presence and of having her guests disturbed by the holidaying ghost. "Whenever he was here, you could smell his cigar smoke. Doors would open and shut in front of you. We would hear the sound of heavy boots walking across the landing overhead and there was a strong sensation of someone - or something - in the room. It was awkward for he continued to use his old room, startling the guests when he opened and closed locked doors. He would stay just for the month. When September came he would arrive and at the end of the month he would disappear again for another year."

The pioneer aviator was an Australian who always flew his biplane from London to the Isle of Wight, landing it at nearby Morton Common. But one September, he crashed-landed and was killed. His ghost was still determined to enjoy its annual holiday and did so, regularly, for a number of years until the Bishop carried out his exorcism.

These rites were a partial success. The pilot hasn't flown back since. But they had no effect on young Andrew, the ghostly child who lingers in the oldest part of the house, which dates back to 1640. He died of diptheria at the age of eight, more than a century ago, but his shade was seen by sensitive guests who stayed at the old farm.

"He is a sweet little lad and he always pays us a visit when we are here," one woman who was a regular visitor for over twenty years, told Graham. "He just stands there in the corner of the room in his nightshirt and smiles at us."

Pepper, a little Jack Russell terrier, which once belonged to Graham's grandfather, is occasionally seen sitting at the top of the stairs near the front door. Killed in an accident with a threshing machine many years ago, Pepper has returned. "I sometimes see him sitting there as I walk through the hall. He has a bent ear, a black patch on one eye and he appears rather like a two-dimensional reflection," said Graham. "We didn't tell our guests that we had the occasional ghost here in case it alarmed them. But most of our regulars knew, and they all loved the warm and friendly atmosphere here ... It certainly drew the pilot back year after year."

More recently, the ghost of a woman in a smock, looking like an old-fashioned dairymaid was seen in the garden of a house in Morton Mews, which was built on the site of the original farmyard at Morton. This spirit has been seen standing in the same spot on a couple of occasions.

"The lady who saw her was at our house recently," said Ann. "When she noticed an old and very grainy photograph we have, she let out a cry. For there, in the picture, was the woman whose ghost she had seen. It was Graham's great, great grandmother, Dora Barnes! She was the first generation of the family to live at Morton."

THE PURITAN'S DOG

When Jack and Paddi Eales took on the job of renovating an eighteenth century stone cottage at Thorley, near Yarmouth, they didn't count on their resident ghost showing such an interest in the work.

They bought Newhouse Cottage in 1969 and over the next decade did their best to overcome the years of neglect it had suffered; delighting in opening up fireplaces; exposing timbers and beams.

As they worked, Jack and Paddi, who were both professional entertainers and cruise directors, became aware that 'something' was watching them.

"We never actually saw anything, but it would be there whenever we were doing major works to the old cottage. The place has a friendly, benign feeling, and whatever is here was very curious and interested in the work. I feel it could be a dog because it seems to be close to the ground. It often sits in a corner behind my chair in the rear sitting room - although we have found it in other rooms where we have been working," Jack said.

Built in 1762, Newhouse Cottage almost certainly replaced a much earlier house; an old stone well in the garden dates from the thirteenth century. Now filled with rubble, it serves as a very damp but desirable abode for an elderly resident toad.

Here, by the old well, late one summer afternoon, Jack caught a glimpse of a spirit who must have died at least three hundred years earlier.

Wearing black Puritan garb, of a high tapering hat, coat with white at the neck, calf-length breeches with white stockings, and black shoes with shiny buckles, he appeared to be walking towards the well.

For a brief moment, he seemed real and quite solid, but then he 'winked-out' leaving Jack standing alone again, with only the chirping of crickets and lazy humming of bees for company.

Newhouse Cottage at Thorley. A Puritan's ghost has been seen here

The long arm of coincidence!

Author's note: While sailing from New York to Southampton aboard Queen Mary 2 in July 2007, I met the internationally-renowned naval historian and fellow author, John Maxtone-Graham.

When I mentioned that I researched and wrote about ghosts on the Isle of Wight, he replied, "I have only been to the Isle of Wight once, and that was in 1980, when I was visiting two friends who worked as cruise directors. I recall they lived in an old cottage near Yarmouth. As we sat in the garden, a dog walked past me into the house. I remarked to my host what a good-looking dog he had. He looked puzzled. 'Our dog died a couple of years ago. You must have seen the ghost-dog we have here'!" And yes, John's old friends on the Island live at Newhouse Cottage, Thorley, and they are Jack and Paddi Eales.

THE DOG'S REVENGE

A little ginger and white Cavalier King Charles spaniel was once the cosseted pet of a young girl, remembered today only as the Blue Lady of Nettlestone. But two centuries ago, they lived and played at Nettlestone Priory, which stands on the site of a medieval building.

A portrait of the young girl, who is believed to have been Esther Grose, once hung in the dining room. She wore a blue dress with a long pointed stomacher and full skirt, trimmed with silver lace. On her wrist perched a canary fastened to one finger by a thin satin ribbon; at her feet frisked the little dog.

Smiling gently, she appeared to be about fourteen or fifteen years old. She died in 1745, shortly after her portrait was painted. When her pet spaniel pined away and died, he was later stuffed and today lies in a glass case at The Priory Bay Hotel (a more detailed account of their story appears in *Original Ghosts of the Isle of Wight*). The Blue Lady, however, continued to love this pet dog from her lonely grave.

In 1927, when the Priory was sold, its furniture and contents were dispersed. The Blue Lady was distraught; her ghost was seen running through the house, sobbing and calling for her lost pet. 'My dog, my dog. What have you done with my dog?' she cried. Servants began to give in their notice.

The new owner, Lady St George, an American socialite, asked why they were leaving. As soon as she heard, the woman started an Islandwide search for the little dog through an advertisement in the local newspaper, finally tracking him down to an antique shop in Newport. Purchasing him for £1, she bore the creature home in triumph, and from that day on, the noises ceased; everything was peaceful again. Today, this fine mansion, set in seventy acres of woodland and landscaped grounds, is an award-winning hotel, which has been run by Andrew and James Palmer since 1997.

Successive owners of The Priory have made sure the little dog is not disturbed, and although the young girl's ghost has been seen over the years, she appears happy. Her shade was spotted in the lounge of the hotel one evening, by a retired gardener. He mistook the ghostly child for a guest and chided her that it was long past her bedtime. In reply, the girl in the long blue dress simply vanished.

Looking a little weary after more than two centuries is the Blue Lady's stuffed dog

Other ghosts walk there still, and a pair of phantom monks has been seen gliding about the grounds. A guest even complained that a ghostly knight in full armour appeared in her room one night.

One foolish (and now former) member of staff at The Priory Bay Hotel scoffed at tales of ghosts and hauntings. He laughed at the story of the Blue Lady and her dog. He took the little spaniel from its resting place to play practical jokes on fellow members of staff; one night, he even put it in someone's bed.

But after the dog's ghost walked across his bedroom floor right in front of him, he never went near it again! He heard the soft patter of a dog's paws on the carpet. Walking across the floor towards him was the ghost of a little Cavalier King Charles spaniel. The room had turned icy cold; the ghost-dog passed him without a second glance, and vanished. "I am convinced the dog was exacting some sort of revenge, punishing me for what I had done and for laughing at its story," he said. "I know better now and there is no way I will ever touch him again."

Curious guests can still ask to see the little dog in his glass case (he is kept in the basement for safety reasons) looking a trifle weary now after two centuries. But does his spirit still frolic with that of the mistress he adored, somewhere beyond the grave? Perhaps...

Visit the Priory Bay Hotel at: *www.priorybay.co.uk*

Chapter Six

HAUNTED CAFES, SHOPS AND NEW HOMES

WATCHER ON THE STAIR

For more than half a century, customers at the Paramount Cafe in Shanklin's Old Village enjoyed meals, snacks or a cup of tea, quite unaware that they may have been sharing a table with Charlie, the cafe ghost. When Josie Jackson bought the business in June 1989 she, too, had no idea that the Paramount was haunted.

In the 1950s the cafe moved with the times becoming the Paramount Milk Bar, but when Josie took over, she renamed it Knights Diner. It was just a couple of weeks after the family moved in that Graham, her youngest son, complained he could hear door handles rattling and someone moving about downstairs in the cafe at night. A quick check confirmed that all the doors and windows were securely locked and bolted. However, someone had made mischief there, because Josie found used coffee grounds and orange juice spilled across the cafe floor. This happened almost every night for the next two weeks. Then, small items such as tea towels would disappear, turning up again weeks later.

Just before Christmas that year, Josie and another son, Andrew, were working late baking batches of mince pies. She recalled, "I told him to go to bed at about 11.30pm and then I set about clearing up. It was while I was washing up at the sink that I started to feel something. The atmosphere changed. The kitchen was becoming colder and colder."

Putting it down to tiredness, Josie began to wash flour from the table. Then suddenly she saw a man dressed in brown standing in front of the cooker, no more than two feet away. He was staring at her.

"I ran out of the kitchen and started to climb the stairs but as I reached the third step, I could go no further. Something was pulling me back. I could not move. It was like one of those awful dreams when you try to run but can't. I could feel hands clutching and gripping my arms, pulling me backwards."

Josie's screams brought Andrew running. "What's the matter mum?" he cried. "You look as though you've seen a ghost!"

They searched the kitchen and checked all the doors, which were locked and bolted. As Josie went up to her bedroom, Andrew came rushing in. He had heard the kitchen door opening and footsteps walking across the tiled floor and up the stairs towards her.

Since that night, Josie always sensed someone - or something - on that third stair. The lights at the top and bottom of the staircase would never stay on. Bulbs failed as soon as they were renewed, and she always kept a torch at both ends of the stairs. "I just couldn't walk up and down there in the dark, and I always talked to myself on that staircase. I would not go up in silence. He was always there, waiting for me, on the third stair."

With the help of Rosemary, a psychic friend, Josie discovered that her watcher on the stair was a ghost named Charlie, who had worked in the building many years earlier. This spirit told Rosemary he had been a 'bit violent' to women during his lifetime. He had once broken a woman's arm in the cafe and wanted to apologise. He had chosen Josie to make his peace with. Would she please listen to him?

Charlie's pleas, however, fell on deaf ears. "I just couldn't do it. I went cold all over when I knew he was there," said Josie.

After Rosemary's visit, Charlie moved even more boldly about the place. One night as she was having a drink with friends in the lounge, Josie felt an unseen hand push her so hard that she spilled her drink.

The café, which was built in the late 1800s on the old garden to Keats Cottage next door, was once a butcher's shop and a wet fish shop. Josie learned that the mother of the previous owner had also been pestered there by 'something'. Perhaps she, too, had been unwilling to accept Charlie's apologies.

From that brief glimpse of Charlie in her kitchen, Josie thought he was aged between 45 and 55, with dark hair and very piercing eyes. "I was caught like a rabbit in headlights, frozen to the spot by those eyes," she said with a shudder.

One September night in 1991, Josie returned home late to find the ghost asleep in a chair in the lounge. A friend who was with her also heard the sound of breathing, and they could both see a figure sprawled in the armchair. "We walked over to the window very quietly, watching him all the time. But as we threw open the curtains, he vanished."

The cafe is a busy fish and chip bar just known as 'The Paramount' now. Josie is no longer there. But what of Charlie, who waited for her on that third stair? Is his ghost bound in some way to the building, held prisoner by his own conscience until he can persuade a woman to accept his apology? Perhaps one day someone will agree to listen and grant forgiveness, delivering him from his long penance.

John Gilbey who runs the Paramount, hasn't seen Charlie yet, although a surprising number of psychic customers tell him that they feel the place is haunted. But he does admit that lots of things 'go missing' in the kitchens. "It's always happening; knives, utensils and kitchen tools vanish all the time. They always reappear eventually. I keep hoping the ghost will do something useful, like peel potatoes or prepare vegetables, but I'm still waiting."

THE HAUNTING OF HILLS

A ghostly shopkeeper continued to count his money at one of Ryde's oldest stores. Hills of Ryde prospered for well over century in imposing Victorian premises in the town's High Street. The site has been occupied for well over 300 years, originally as an inn, The Nagg's Head, where once the author, Henry Fielding, took rooms.

Fielding set sail for Lisbon in June 1754, but was forced to go ashore at Ryde for almost two weeks to wait for more favourable winds. He describes being carried ashore by two sailors, wading through the mud on the seashore, and being conveyed to The Nagg's Head, where the landlady, Mrs Francis, grudgingly provided food and lodging for Fielding, his wife and servants, overcharging them for everything!

Fielding wrote, *"Mrs Francis was a short squat woman; her head was closely joined to her shoulders, where it was fixed, somewhat awry; every feature of her countenance was sharp and pointed; her face was furrowed with the small-pox, and her complexion seemed able to turn milk to curds."*

Later the site was used by a blacksmith, baker, butcher, grocer and house agent, before becoming Hill and Co, drapers, in the 1890s. Over the years, staff whispered tales of ghosts, but when Tony, an electrician for the Southern Electricity Board, was sent to the store on a wiring job in 1962, he had no idea the shop was haunted.

Tony and his partner were busy in the front of the premises late one Thursday afternoon. It was early-closing day and apart from the two workmen, the shop was empty; the doors locked. Then came the sound of a bag full of money being tipped onto a glass-topped counter. "It was a very odd, distinctive noise, and my mate walked over to the old cash-desk nearby to see what had caused it," said Tony." He came shooting back, his hair standing on end, and said there was absolutely nothing there. The old shop suddenly felt icy cold, and I rushed for the front door, forgetting it was locked."

The two men told themselves they had been imagining things, but half-an-hour later came the sound of a baby's rattle being shaken. In the nearby children's department, they discovered a rattle lying on the counter. "That was it. We had had enough surprises for one afternoon. We unlocked the doors and were off," confessed Tony.

Peter Jones, who became manager of Hills in 1964, recalled the day one of his customers vanished – literally into thin air. So did Ray Harvey who was working with Peter at the time. "She was a little elderly lady wearing a long black coat and a black straw hat. Queer old-fashioned clothes they were," said Peter.

The strange little customer asked Peter for some pillows, and as he went to fetch them, she disappeared. She was the only customer in the store that lunchtime but no one ever saw her leave…

The store is now closed. The upper floors, once the furniture and carpet departments, are now residential flats, while the Ryde Jobcentre occupies the ground floor. Staff there are aware of the haunting stories, but report that the ghosts are quiet – for now at least.

HAUNTED COUNCIL HOUSE

A house doesn't have to be old or historic to have a ghost. Many of the following hauntings occur in newly built homes...

When Judy Axford and her son Darren, aged nine, moved into their newly-built house overlooking Wootton Creek, owned by the local authority, they never dreamt it came with a ghost.

Psychic ability and a sensitivity to the supernatural run in Judy's family (another of her experiences is told elsewhere in this book) but the two-bedroom house in Mary Rose Avenue looked and felt normal. Then, one evening at about 9pm, when Judy and Darren were sitting in the lounge watching television, she glanced up to see the figure of a tall man appear in the fireplace and walk across the room - *through* the chairs.

Not wanting to frighten her son, she suppressed any exclamation of surprise, but Darren had seen it too. "He sat there with his mouth wide open looking as if he had seen a ghost. Which of course he had."

The boy asked, "Did you see that, mum? It was a man, wasn't it?" The figure, which appeared solid, was very tall but moved with a shuffle, as though leaning on a walking stick. The following day Judy discovered her scissors were missing; her next-door neighbour was puzzled to find a pile of hair cuttings sitting in the middle of her dining room table. Together they made a thorough search of both houses and discovered the scissors were upstairs in the neighbour's jewellery box.

This was the only strange thing ever to happen in that house, but it left Judy, Darren and their neighbour bemused and wondering to this day, just whose hair was it?

A Disembodied Hand

Meanwhile in a house opposite, Marilyn Allen and her family also experienced ghostly 'goings on' in their home, which was built at the same time as Judy's. When they first saw the house, they knew it was for them. "It was like being cuddled when you came in; we loved it," Marilyn said. Whatever shared the house with them was not malevolent, although it once gave her son Davis, then eight, the fright of his life. Marilyn was often aware of a man's presence in the house, and his figure was seen on the landing and stairs.

The first time it appeared, Marilyn was sitting in the lounge watching television with Davis, when a man's hand materialised on the stair rail. A white shape, at least six feet tall, walked across the hall into the kitchen wall and vanished. Marilyn could actually see the front door through the figure.

She looked at Davis, who was just staring after it, and asked him what he had seen. "It was a white man. But why could I see through him, Mummy?" the puzzled boy replied.

One night shortly after Christmas in 1991, Davis went upstairs to get ready for bed. Suddenly he rushed downstairs in such a panic that he was unable to speak. He was petrified and shaking. Between sobs, Davis said he had been looking for his pyjamas, when a disembodied hand and arm came floating towards him.

It was a man's right hand and on the wrist was an old-fashioned watch with a brown leather strap. Davis refused to go upstairs on his own for weeks after this.

THE GHOST WORE A TEE-SHIRT

Meanwhile, in the adjoining house, Megan and Malcolm Scambell kept losing things; little things; keys; earrings and especially clothes. A drawer full of Megan's tee shirts vanished for several weeks. "We turned the house upside down. We searched everywhere. Then one day they were back. I couldn't believe it," Megan said.

Her family lived at the house since it was built in the early 1980s, and her mother, Dilys Ennion, recalls that from the time they moved in, things would disappear. A nurse's silver belt buckle was gone for weeks; keys would vanish from their pegs. No one saw them move, but move they did.

Whatever shared their home never materialised. It simply borrowed things. "You could put something down one minute, turn round and it would be gone. We just got used to it; everything always turned up again - eventually," Malcolm said.

A SHY SPIRIT

When Mark Grabham went with his parents to view the council's show house at Mary Rose Avenue, the family immediately knew it was the one for them. As they moved in a few weeks later, even George, the resident ghost, turned out to welcome them.

On only the second day there, Mark saw the ghost at the top of the stairs. "I never felt frightened of him. He was almost like a guardian spirit," said Mark.

The following June, Mark lost his car keys, lighter and tobacco tin. He hunted everywhere, only to find them, weeks later in the pocket of a coat he had not worn for months. "I was certain this was George trying to attract my attention." Then the ghost started to appear about the house. He wore a black jacket with a hat and carried a walking cane. An elderly ghost who appeared to be in his sixties, George was quite spry, and seemed to enjoy pop music, especially rock and roll.

"Often when I was up in my room listening to the radio or record player, the door would open and I would sense him there with me. I never really got a good look at his face. He seemed shy, fading in and out whenever I looked."

All the family, including the dog, saw and heard George. Even Mark's wife chatted to him one day, thinking it was her husband who had just walked upstairs and into the bedroom. It wasn't!

PHANTOMS FROM THE BLITZ

The answer to this unusual level of ghostly activity in such a new housing development lay beneath the homes. Some of the ground there was very wet, for underground streams feed the nearby lake and Wootton

Creek. Tons of hardcore and rubble were laid down before the houses were built. The land was so marshy that a tractor sank during the work.

During the last war, many houses in Cowes and East Cowes were destroyed or damaged. In a single devastating air raid on May 5th 1942, seventy men, women and children were killed in the two towns. A further eighty were seriously injured.

Barry Abraham of Kite Hill Farm, Wootton, confirmed that some of the rubble from those homes was dumped and lay forgotten at an old brickyard in Whippingham, until it was finally used as infill under the foundations of those first houses to be built at the lower end of Mary Rose Avenue. Are all the hauntings there related; connected in some strange way with those tragic deaths more than 60 years ago?

Marilyn believed they were, and that one of those killed in the bombing was a man who wore an old-fashioned round-faced watch with a brown leather strap.

HAUNTED NEWLY-WEDS

When their local GP refused to set foot in their flat because it had a ghost, a young East Cowes couple realised they had a problem.

In 1967, newly-weds David and Jennifer Godfrey rented a ground floor flat in the rambling red-brick Victorian villa in York Avenue as their first home. Now living in Sandown, the couple recall paying rent of three guineas a week for their old flat.

"It was a nice place and we liked it. Originally built for one of Queen Victoria's ladies-in-waiting, it was a very grand house with cellars, high ceilings and huge ten-foot square windows," said Jennifer.

The first intimation that something was wrong came when David was in the flat on his own, a few weeks before the wedding. He was awoken by a thunderous knocking on the front door, at 4am one morning. Reaching the door, he could feel the vibrations from the heavy cast iron knocker. But when he opened it, the noise stopped abruptly.

No one was there. The front porch was empty and although he searched around, there was no sign of anyone in the grounds. Puzzled, David looked again, thinking someone must have been playing a trick, but found no string tied to the knocker.

After the wedding, some months later, Jennifer woke one night to see a figure moving at the bottom of the bed. She called out, thinking it was David. But he was watching television in the next room. The figure was

Old Newport Villa at East Cowes was haunted by a woman in a long hooded cloak

wearing a long grey hooded cape. Jennifer saw it nod its head, as if acknowledging her.

Another morning, again at 4am, David saw the same figure float past the bed. As he watched in amazement, it glided across the foot of the bed and disappeared out of the window.

"I was terrified. I just ducked down under the covers until it had gone," he admitted.

Shortly afterwards, a neighbour from upstairs knocked at their door in a terrible state one morning. "He just stood there pointing, too shocked to speak. He was as white as a sheet and babbled that he had just seen a ghost. We got him inside and sat him down. He told us that a woman in a grey cloak had floated out of our bedroom window and disappeared into the ground near the basement," David said.

It seems that other people in East Cowes knew of Newport Villa's strange reputation, for when the Godfreys signed on with a local GP, this doctor warned them not to expect him to make any home visits. And true to his word, he never did.

Newport Villa was demolished in 1988 and the site has since been redeveloped. But what became of that hooded grey lady? Does she continue to glide through a window that is no longer there?

Chapter Seven

VICTORIAN GHOSTS AND HAUNTED SCHOOLS

THE HAUNTING HOUSEKEEPER

A Victorian ghost named Violet appointed herself 'keeper of the house' at Lower Knighton Farm, Newchurch, where she was often accompanied by a strong scent of the flower after which she was named.

When the Newnham family moved there in 1984, they became accustomed to Violet popping up all over the house, and Angela Newnham often passed the time of day with her, calling out 'Good morning Violet' whenever she sensed the shade entering the room. Angela, a psychic and a registered healer, was often aware of Violet following her about the house.

Built in 1747 on the site of an earlier dwelling, the farm was once occupied by the bailiff to the nearby (haunted) Knighton Gorges estate. The site was visible from the old farmhouse, and sometimes on a still, clear night, the sound of a horse and carriage was heard rumbling up the narrow winding lane. Angela never saw this carriage, but late one night she heard the ghostly horses neighing and snorting so clearly that she got out of bed to look, convinced that her own horses were loose.

Angela and Gary, her builder husband, renovated the old farmhouse, restoring original features faithfully - which evidently met with Violet's approval. Gary encountered Violet only once, when he was working alone in the house, opening up the old fireplace. The dining room suddenly went icy cold and he was so scared that when Angela came home, she found he had barricaded himself in their bedroom.

The dining room, with its 20inch thick walls, central heating and large open fire, should have been a warm room, but visitors constantly remarked how cold it was. Angela simply explained that this was where Violet lived.

"All we really knew about Violet was that she lived here during the 19th century when she was the housekeeper for Squire Carter and his family, and she considered herself still the 'keeper' of Lower Knighton Farm. I never saw her clearly but just caught odd glimpses of her. She was always wearing a little muslin or lace bag of herbs and sweet-smelling perfume pinned to the bodice of her gown."

Apart from an irritating habit of moving small articles such as keys around the house, Violet was a benign ghost. "She was extremely kind and tried to help me. We got on very well and it was often like having an invisible friend about the place."

Ivy Welstead, who was also a medium, clearly remembered Violet and her activities. "I always knew when she was about, for there would be a strong smell of Parma violets in the room," said Ivy with a smile. She and her family lived at the farm for 18 years, and during the last war they felt Violet was keeping them safe. "I saw her clearly on several occasions. She always wore a long, tight-waisted black dress with little black jet buttons down the front. She stood with her hands folded and her hair, medium brown I think, was rolled into a tight bun. She would look at me and smile. Violet favoured the parlour and would often stand in the corner of the dining room, doing what she had always done during her life ... keeping house."

When the present owners of Lower Knighton Farm, bought the house in 1995 they were aware of its haunting history. Violet, however, seems to have made herself scarce and the family report that all is presently quiet there.

LACE-TRIMMED PETTICOAT

Ghosts can, and do, turn up in the oddest, most unexpected, and occasionally embarrassing, places. Linzi Mathews would be the first to agree with this. A ghost appeared to her one day at work - when she was sitting on the loo!

The unforgettable incident happened in 1982, when Linzi, who at the time worked for the Department of Health and Social Security at Broadlands House, went to the ladies' toilets on the first floor. "I was sitting there, contemplating the floor, when I saw a foot appear at the bottom of the door. However, there was no gap; the door went all the way to the floor. The foot was clad in a small, old-fashioned, pointed lady's shoe in dark grey, decorated with buttons. Above the shoe I could see the hem of a lace petticoat," said Linzi.

"It was as though the rest of the lady was standing on the other side of the door and she had just stepped forward. I didn't dare to open the cubicle door in case she really was there. I saw her foot for only a few seconds, and after it vanished, I could still feel her presence, but when I did pluck up the courage to look, the room was empty."

Linzi no longer works at Broadlands House, but when she told colleagues what had happened, she discovered that the Broadlands ghost had been seen, heard and even smelled over the years. The strong aroma of toasting bread would sometimes waft through the corridors, a faint echo of an afternoon tea party long ago, perhaps. Late in the afternoon, staff working in the upper part of the old house, sometimes heard footsteps echoing in empty rooms, and the sound of knocking, and furniture moving on the top landing.

Old Broadlands House lace factory at Newport

Broadlands House at Newport, was once Nunn's Lace Factory, one of the biggest employers on the Island, with almost 200 men, women, boys and girls working there. The factory was established in 1827 by Mr. H.W. Nunn and George Freeman, and was soon making enormous profits through selling French blonde lace. Queen Victoria and other ladies of the court were among its customers. This special lace was as fine as a spider web and very costly, but sales were dependent on the fickle fashion industry. By 1870, old Mr. Nunn retired and with no son to take on the business, it was closed down, the machinery was sold off, and many poor people found themselves thrown out of work. For some of them, the Workhouse was the only option.

With the demise of the lace industry, the old factory - in a timely fashion became Broadlands House Home - a charitable establishment for forty 'poor spinsters and widow ladies who had fallen on hard times'. Established in 1880 by Mary Nunn Harvey who inherited Broadlands, the charity also helped to train young working-class girls as servants to be placed in service around the town.

Tragically, one of these girls was killed in a fire there in January 1904. Alice Barton, aged 14, had been left alone in the matron's sitting room, when she stood on the fender of the fireplace to look at some papers on the mantelpiece. A red-hot ember dropped from the fire onto her dress and the fabric quickly ignited. Her injuries were so severe that she died at Broadlands House. The home closed for good in the 1930s, and in 1949, it was bought by the Ministry of Labour. Although it has been extensively altered over the years, the old house still retains traces of its former glory. Today, it is incorporated in the Department of Work and Pensions at Staplers Road. By day, this busy complex is full of people, and no ghosts are seen. But early in the mornings and late afternoons, when the building is deserted, some staff do sense a presence there still.

So, whose foot did Linzi see and who is the Broadlands ghost enjoying her buttered toast in the afternoon? Was she a distressed gentlewomen fallen on hard times or the unfortunate Alice Barton who died in the fire? And Linzi still wonders if the petticoat she glimpsed was trimmed with Isle of Wight lace.

TRAGEDY AT NEWCHURCH

The 300-year-old schoolhouse at Langbridge in Newchurch, has had many generations of village children through its doors. There, under the watchful eye of the resident schoolmaster, they learned to read, to write and do sums. But by 1876, the little school was redundant. Replaced by a larger elementary school, it became a private residence.

But the old schoolhouse was haunted. Tragedy has struck at least twice in its history; the bodies of children were found in an ancient, stone-lined well nearby. Coroner's records for 1384 show that an inquest was held into the death of two-year-old Ellen Couherd who 'fell into a well at Langbridge'. Her distraught mother, Juliana, found her body.

Centuries later, the little stone schoolhouse was built nearby on land donated by General Bocland, the owner of Knighton Gorges. It consisted of 'a large school-room with a residence for the master, and a garden. The whole number of scholars being about 30.'

A further tragedy cast a shadow over village life in 1747, when an inquest was held into the death of another child found in the Langbridge well. This time the verdict was murder. The man responsible was a relative of Elizabeth Poell, the young victim, who was about nine or ten-years-old. He was sent for trial at the Winchester Assize in the following year, where he paid with his own life for the wicked deed.

The village Poor Book records that five shillings was spent in searching for the girl's strangled and battered body; James Poell was 'carried to jail' at a cost of two pounds. Further details of the murder are

Old School House Cottage, once the Newchurch village school, is pictured in 1992

lost in the mists of time, but the little girl's shade may have lingered in the old school, as did the ghost of a man in dark clothing, who was seen and heard in a bedroom and in the lane outside - close to the old well.

The former schoolhouse is now a charming pair of semi-detached cottages, Puckaster Cottage and Old School House Cottage. Until the late 1970s, Elizabeth Green lived there with Lizzie, her daughter, who had Down's syndrome. Locked into childhood herself, Lizzie, spent many happy hours sitting in the garden on her swing, and on the landing upstairs, talking to her 'friend', a little girl whom no one else could see.

Old School House Cottage was bought in 1964 by builder Dave Cotton, who, during renovation works, uncovered ancient beams on which generations of Newchurch children had carved their names. He also found an old bread oven in the schoolhouse kitchen and discovered an ancient well outside the kitchen door. It was here that Judy Axford had a terrifying experience, which she still vividly recalls. Judy's story begins one winter's night in 1980, when she called to see Dave.

The Dragging in the Darkness

He wasn't at home so Judy waited in her little Hillman Imp car in the lane nearby. As she sat in the dark, she heard a curious dragging sound, coming from further down the lane in the marshland behind. "It was as if something heavy was being pulled along the ground. I peered into the darkness but saw nothing," she said. "As I sat in my car, the dragging sound moved alongside, and stopped. I strained my ears. Then came a hoarse, throaty gurgle. It was horrible. It sounded as if someone was being choked to death - or strangled right beside me.

"Oddly, the image of stockings came into my mind. I was so terrified that I just started the car and shot off up the lane so fast that I almost wrecked the engine. That sound was so loud, so inexplicable, that my hair stood up on end. I was terrified and couldn't get away fast enough."

Several months later, when Judy lived at the cottage, she had another strange experience there. "I was aware of a presence and cold spots, and I had the feeling that I was never totally alone there," she recalls.

At 10.30pm one October night, Judy witnessed another chapter from the cottage's dark past. "I was reading in bed, when suddenly I looked up to find a dark figure in a large square-brimmed hat standing by the bedroom window. It glided towards my bed, and then disappeared. I had half-been expecting something to happen, because there was always that sensation of 'something' there with me," she said.

Judy turned back to her book and then, surprisingly, she quickly fell asleep. She was woken at 2am by the sound of a man's rapid and heavy breathing coming from the side of her bed where the figure had vanished earlier. "I held my own breath for a few seconds and listened. The room was freezing cold, and I was very frightened indeed. I realised that whatever I had seen earlier, had returned.

"I'll never know where I found the strength to get out of bed and turn the light on. I ran out onto the landing, switched on the light there, and made for the stairs to the attic where Dave was sleeping. Suddenly, the landing light went out. I felt like I was moving in slow motion; I tried to run up those narrow wooden stairs so quickly that I ended crawling up on all fours. I burst into Dave's room only to find him fast asleep."

Judy sobbed out her story, trying to convince Dave she had just seen a ghost in her room. "I grabbed his arm and wouldn't let go. As Dave came downstairs with me, the landing light went on again. My bedroom felt like ice. It was full of chilled air, just as if someone had opened the door of a deep-freeze. Then as we stood there, the light went out."

Judy never used that room again; she insisted on sleeping on the settee downstairs in the lounge instead. "My old room always felt cold after that night, and I always slept with the downstairs lights on. Often, as I moved through the cottage, lights switched themselves off after me."

As the year ended, Judy had yet another brush with the supernatural at Old School House. Shortly after midnight on New Year's Eve, she went to the back door to call her cats in. "Suddenly there was a tremendous clatter as a carriage, or horse and cart, rushed past me. I could hear the horses' hooves, their harness creaking and the sound of the wheels in the lane. But nothing was there. It was very cold, but I had no sense of air moving past. I was so shocked and terrified that I screamed. It was a scream from the very depths of my being. I frightened myself with the noise."

In 1995, David Phillips and Daphne Hayles bought Old School House Cottage, while Moyra Trott, David's sister, moved into Puckaster Cottage next door. "We were aware that the place was haunted, but so far it has been pretty quiet here," David said.

However, both he and Daphne have heard phantom footsteps walking above their heads in the empty attic, while, next door, Moyra occasionally notices the very distinctive smell of old-fashioned but ghostly tobacco smoke.

OLD WROXALL SCHOOL GHOST

For over a century, generations of Wroxall children learned their three R's at the little Victorian village school. But how many realised they were sharing their lessons with the school ghost?

The old building, which celebrated its centenary in 1973, was demolished 13 years later and its 100 pupils and staff moved into a purpose-built primary school nearby. New homes went up in place of classrooms and playgrounds, and ever since, villagers who went to the old school have wondered what became of their ghost. Few were ever frightened; it was an accepted part of school life. Some of them even claimed to have seen the presence 'lurking' in the old toilet block.

Mike Davis, who became Headteacher of Wroxall Primary School in 1980, was convinced the old school was haunted. He heard footsteps in empty classrooms; furniture being moved late at night, and felt there was always a presence around.

"I was never alone in the place. Someone or something else was there with me. There were several cold spots, which could be quite unpleasant, and I always disliked locking up in the dark, at night. I would feel most uncomfortable and couldn't get out fast enough.

The old, and haunted, Wroxall Primary School was demolished in 1986

Even my dog refused to go into some parts of that school."

Elderly villagers believed the ghost was a workman who fell from scaffolding to his death, when the school was being built. Mike confirmed that the presence always felt stronger in the infant and junior classroom and an upstairs room. This feeling became overwhelming the day Mike gave the children a glimpse of the past with a special 'Victorian Day'. "They all came to school in Victorian-style clothes; I dressed as their schoolmaster and we had an old-fashioned lesson using the blackboard and writing slates.

"The atmosphere that day was most extraordinary and very powerful. The school felt quite weird, as if we had somehow evoked the past. I never tried it again."

School secretary Chris Mogg, who joined the staff in 1972, also heard those footsteps walking across an old wooden classroom floor when the building was locked and in darkness. "To me, the presence had an impish, almost mischievous feel, and it made me uneasy," she said. "The old school was lovely during the day when it was filled with happy children. But when it was empty, it was a different place, and not a comfortable one. I was not at all sorry it was pulled down," Chris added.

(Read other stories of haunted schools in *Even More Ghosts*)

Chapter Eight

POLTERGEISTS, GHOST SHIPS AND SPIRITS AT SEA

THE MAGPIE POLTERGEIST

Whatever shared Veniscombe House at Newchurch with Ian and Sue Debrett had a magpie-like fascination for shiny gold objects and jewellery. The missing items turned up again eventually, sometimes years after they disappeared. The ghost was no thief however; it simply liked to borrow things.

It was only their ghost's light-fingered tendencies that caused annoyance. A new belt of Ian's, with a gold buckle, was lost for several weeks. This reappeared coiled in the middle of the very chair from which it had vanished. Sue once lost a favourite gold medallion and after searching high and low, she thought it had gone for good. However, five years later when carpets were being taken up during redecoration works, the medallion was found in the middle of the bedroom floor...underneath a heavy carpet.

Sue never saw the ghost in the 30 years they lived there, although she heard it countless times. She and Ian grew used to the three sharp raps on the front door, which could happen any time of the day or night.

Sue often heard footsteps on the landings when the house was empty, and when her children were young, she would often run upstairs, ready to tell them to get back to bed, only to find them fast asleep. Whatever had been scurrying around upstairs, it certainly wasn't her children.

"Sometimes I would stand in the kitchen and feel tiny hands plucking at my skirt at toddler level, but there was never anything there. We just learned to accept such things. There was nothing frightening there, it was actually rather nice," said Sue.

That's not what Ian said when he discovered the ghost had switched off their washing machine and an enormous chest freezer. This happened several times, and it was impossible for the switches to have been knocked accidentally. "It was a deliberate act and happened twice as I actually walked into the room. That freezer felt like it weighed a ton as I had to pull it out from the wall to reach the switches."

Ian was certain that Veniscombe's ghost was male. Significantly, an entry in the Newchurch Coroner's Roll for 1377 shows that a local man,

John Grontale, was killed with a knife during a struggle in a field at Fenycombe (Veniscombe). Could it be his earthbound spirit there?

Penny Staines and her partner David bought Veniscombe in 2004. They love its warm and welcoming feel (many years ago the annual church fetes were held in its

Stone from the haunted mansion of Knighton Gorges was used to build Veniscombe House in Newchurch

gardens). They discovered that the present house was built by Squire William Thatcher, the owner of Wacklands Farm for two of his spinster daughters in 1826. Squire Thatcher, 'a small man with a big voice and red face' was acknowledged as probably the most prominent sportsman and huntsman on the Island, as well as being a 'fine judge of port wine'. Cock fighting was his passion and he kept more than forty game cocks. The fights took place in a barn at Hale Common (near the Fighting Cocks Inn). The purse for some fights was as much as 100 guineas. Squire Thatcher died in 1845, aged 65, and is buried at Newchurch.

Veniscombe was built using stone, and undoubtedly other materials, salvaged from the ancient mansion of nearby Knighton Gorges, which was pulled down in 1821.

Neither Penny nor David has yet lost any valuables. Shortly after moving in however, Penny heard footsteps when she was alone and sensed a presence there with her. "I did not like being on my own when we first came here, but that feeling has now lifted," she said.

And with their little dog, Otis, (named after Otis lifts - because he jumps up and down a lot) bouncing around, no ghost would be able to pilfer anything from Veniscombe now!

THE GHOST WHO LIKED CHOCOLATE CAKE

Whatever haunted the old Clarendon Hotel and Wight Mouse Inn at Chale had an impish sense of humour and a particular fondness for ham sandwiches and chocolate cake. Until they sold up in 1998, Jean and John Bradshaw lived at the old 17th century coaching inn, turning it one of the Island's most popular hostelries and winning Egon Ronay's Family Pub of the Year accolade.

Years earlier the previous owners, Pat and Norman Stagg, had warned the Bradshaws about an old sailor who haunted the place; adding that his bent and bearded figure appeared on the top landing upstairs. "We didn't really take them seriously," said Jean. "But after we moved in, we knew there was definitely something here."

At that time, only Jean and John and their two children, James and Sally, lived on the premises. Jean would wake at 6.30am to get the children ready for school and start preparing the bar food.

One morning, while the children were having their cereal, Jean packed James's lunch-box with a ham sandwich, a slice of chocolate cake, apple and crisps, and put it out on the worktop for him. The school bus arrived and James asked his mum for his packed-lunch. But he never took it to school that day; it had vanished. James left empty-handed, and later that morning Jean drove to Ventnor with more sandwiches and cake for him. "I was furious. I knew I had made his lunch that day and put it ready. I hadn't even left the kitchen. It was a complete mystery but the fact was, it had disappeared."

Two months later, Jean decided to clear out several huge chest freezers full of cooked food, which she had inherited from Pat. The locked freezers were in a locked utility room outside, and Jean had never opened them. "I started to empty the stuff out. There, at the very bottom of a freezer, buried under mountains of food, was the missing lunch-box. I couldn't believe my eyes. Everything was still in it and frozen solid. How it got there was a complete and utter mystery. We all laughed about it, but it was rather frightening at the time."

As the family settled down in their new home, they grew accustomed to things going missing. Keys would disappear almost as soon as they were put down. Ornaments were moved, and sometimes in the morning, Jean would come downstairs to find furniture had been changed around during the night.

"He isn't malicious, just friendly and mischievous. When the business took off and became really busy, he went quiet. Perhaps it was all too much for him and he moved on to find somewhere quieter where his pranks will be appreciated," Jean said.

In 1905, author Hubert Garle wrote, "*In the village of Chale is a comfortable little hotel called the Clarendon, where everything is clean and the charges moderate – three recommendations that cannot be given to all hotels on the Island. I found an agreeable welcome in the shape of a hot supper awaiting me. So mild was the atmosphere that I breakfasted in the open air – and this in December. For anyone suffering from insomnia, doctors advise Chale as the antidote."*

Today, the Clarendon ghost may not recognise his old haunt, indeed the current licensees report that he is quiet now. The Wight Mouse Inn has been extended and altered, almost beyond recognition, into a popular and busy family-friendly pub with a reputation for good food. There is seating for 265 diners indoors and tables in the gardens for 250 more. Its guest bedrooms have views over the wild and sweeping coastline 'Back of the Wight'.

Visit the White Mouse at: *www.innforanight.co.uk*

THE BAY OF DEATH

The little inn was originally called The White Mouse, but took the name of Clarendon following one of the most infamous shipwrecks of the 19th century, when it was enlarged using timbers from the wreck. Chale Bay was then known - with good reason - as the 'Bay of Death'. With no lighthouse and a lee shore, it made a perfect graveyard for countless unfortunate ships.

The Clarendon, a three-masted 345-ton ship, under Captain Samuel Walker, left St Kitts in the West Indies on August 27th 1836, carrying a cargo of sugar, molasses and rum, with ten passengers and 16 crew.

Battered by strong Atlantic gales, storms forced her towards Portsmouth. By dusk on October 10th, the Clarendon was in serious trouble. In hurricane force winds, the ship was pushed towards the Blackgang shore, unable to fight her way back to sea. The situation on board was desperate.

At 6am on October 11th, the ship turned sideways to the waves and hit the beach, rolling on to her side. The huge waves made short work of the Clarendon, tearing her apart in less than 15 minutes. From the shore, local fishermen helplessly watched the tragedy unfold.

Then, one of them, John Wheeler, a former man-o-war sailor, did an astonishingly brave thing. He fastened a stout rope around his middle and jumped into the waves. Wheeler crashed into the surf twice, and each time returned with a crewman. Another man made it to shore but he was the last to do so alive. Only the second mate and two sailors were saved. All the passengers were lost; either drowned or dashed to death, among them a family of six, consisting of Lieutenant Shore of the 14th Regiment, his wife Louisa and their four daughters, aged from nine months to 18 years. (Mrs Shore's brother

The old Clarendon public bar pictured in 1949

lived in Newport, so the family was interred in Church Litten cemetery on 13th October). The battered, naked bodies of thirteen sailors and nine passengers, their clothing ripped off by the seas, were swept ashore at Chale, where most were buried at St Andrew's Churchyard. (Years ago, Reverend Sinclair, Vicar of Chale, who rode around on a tricycle wearing a billowing black cloak, was one of the investigators of notorious Borley Rectory, known as 'the most haunted house in England'. Read of a phantom funeral at the church in *Ghosts of the Isle of Wight Book Three*)

Of the final passenger however, there was no trace. In an almost unbelievable and bizarre 'coincidence', the body of Miss Gourlay of Portsmouth was carried away on the tide, only to be washed ashore on the beach at Southsea, at the foot of a garden belonging to her father, Captain Gourlay RN.

The wreck of the Clarendon and the public death of women and young children only yards from the shore made a huge impact on the public consciousness at the time. For years, demands for a lighthouse near Niton had been ignored. But as a result of the disaster, work on St Catherine's Lighthouse was started in 1837 and completed in 1840, to help prevent further loss of life. (See a photograph of the lighthouse ghost and read of hauntings there in *Most Haunted Island*)

BOULDNOR'S GHOSTLY GALLEON

A ghostly galleon under full sail was seen one summer night by a couple fishing at Bouldnor, near Yarmouth. Julie Matthews and husband Geoff could hardly believe their eyes when the vessel came so close inshore that they felt they could almost touch it.

Julie, a local JP, has often listened to some far-fetched stories when sitting in court. "But this was so strange I can still hardly believe it happened to us," she said. "We had lit a fire on the beach; it was a lovely clear night, and the fish were biting well, when we noticed an old three-masted ship, like the Mary Rose, out at sea. There were flickering lanterns on the masts and at the bow and stern."

As the couple watched with concern, the vessel sailed closer and closer to shore right in front of them. But rather than running aground, it slowly disappeared. As dawn broke on an empty beach, they knew for certain it was no real ship they had seen, but a ghost, for no vessel of that size could have sailed so close to the shore.

This sighting was in the summer of 1978, some years before the blackened timbers of a mystery vessel were first discovered in 1984 during an archaeological survey of the seabed off Yarmouth.

Initially, only a few centimetres of timber was showing, but it was soon realised that this was an important site and the wreck was designated as a Protected Wreck site. The ship has since been identified as the sixteenth century Spanish carrack, the Santa Lucia, which ran aground 'athwart Yarmouthe' after being crippled in bad weather close to the shore. So close in fact, according to former County Archaeologist Dr David Tomalin, that her three masts would have been visible even at high tide, until the vessel, which may have resembled Christopher Columbus's flagship the Santa Maria, eventually broke up. Although the cargo was salvaged at the time, many artefacts were later excavated from the site. The Santa Lucia, which was over 30 metres long, was on her way to Flanders in 1567 with a cargo of wool. The ship 'perished and was lost in the seas thwart of Yarmouthe, in the Isle of Wight'.

Almost five centuries later, her remains lie covered in the mud and silt of the Solent. But Julie and Geoff still wonder why her ghost should have appeared to them that night.

PHANTOM WRECKS

Further round the coast 'Back of the Wight' lurks the notorious Atherfield Ledge, which over the centuries, has claimed countless ships and hundreds of lives. These treacherous rocks, just half a mile square, occupy a deadly position in Atherfield Bay where an extraordinary number of vessels have gone down in this ships' graveyard.

Their ghosts are still seen, sailing again and again to their doom, and fishermen tell strange tales of hauntings on those lonely beaches. A century ago, Islanders living along that stretch of coast swore that on certain nights they saw a phantom Revenue ship pass by.

More recently, one starlit summer's night as former schoolteacher Robin Ford and several friends were enjoying a barbecue on the beach, they noticed a three-masted sailing ship drifting ashore in Compton Bay. Outlined by lanterns, the old vessel kept heading for the beach. When it was just a few yards from shore, the lights started to go out; then the ship went down, bow first.

AN AURA OF SADNESS AND LONGING

During World War Two, there was a strong Army presence around Brighstone to defend the Island from invasion. Dugouts, pillboxes, and sea defences of barbed wire and long, scaffold-type poles protected the coast; local beaches were out of bounds to civilians. Anti-aircraft guns were positioned on the Military Road. Up to 1,000 troops were billeted in Brighstone Holiday Camp, others camped on the Downs, while nearby, officers occupied Sea Breeze, a wooden hotel built in the 1930s.

In the early hours of the morning on April 17th 1942, a German bomber dropped a flare above Brighstone's pre-war holiday camp and followed this up with three high explosive bombs, which hit and demolished Sea Breeze. Ten men were killed that night, and the spirit of at least one of these unfortunate men did not rest easy.

Ten men were killed here at Sea Breeze when it was bombed in April 1942

Some thirty years later, Barney's Roadhouse was built on the derelict site of that old hotel. Julie Clifton, who ran the pub, restaurant and nightspot for seven years until 1992, confirmed that it was haunted.

Julie, who subsequently managed the Earl Mountbatten Hospice Shop in Newport, heard stories about the ghosts at Barney's from regular customers, but she always dismissed them as nonsense - until one Thursday morning when she was alone in the cellar there and felt a phantom hand stroking her face.

Julie was standing in the middle of the cellar. There were no curtains or cobwebs nearby. "A cold wisp of cloudy substance brushed slowly past my cheek. It stroked me as though it just wanted to touch my skin," said Julie. "There was a real feeling of sadness and longing in the air."

After that, she never again dismissed claims by customers and staff that they, too, had seen or felt a ghost there at that lonely roadside pub.

Barney's Roadhouse closed in the 1990s, when the site was re-developed as Sea Breeze Holiday Cottages.

THEY WALK THE BEACHES

Through the long days of summer, only sun worshippers haunt the beaches of Compton, Brook and Atherfield. But when the sun goes down, those same beaches take on a darker and more sinister aspect.

The 'Back of the Wight' was once the haunt of smugglers, wreckers and 'free traders'. There is scarcely a cove or chine where tubs of contraband have not come ashore secretly, at dead of night. So, is it the ghost of a long-dead smuggler or a shipwrecked sailor who walks the lonely beaches between Blackgang, Atherfield and Chale?

Some local anglers won't fish alone there at night. They have seen and heard strange things, and talk of their experiences only with reluctance. Peter Shortman of Whitwell fished from those beaches for years, but one night he caught more than he bargained for. "I was in a little cove on my own near Atherfield Point. I saw a man come around the point. He was dressed in a long black jacket, an old sailor's cap, and he had boots and seaman's socks on."

By the light of his Tilley lamp, Peter could just make out the seaman's features. He was in his fifties, with a beard. "As he went past I said, 'How do.' He just looked at me and nodded. I could hear the crunch of his footsteps as he walked off across the shingle beach. Then it dawned on me. The tide was in and he could not have come round the point. He had walked out of the sea, but his feet were dry."

Another lone fisherman saw a figure in black nearby. As he stood at the water's edge, this angler saw and heard someone running towards him. The figure was dressed in black and as it neared him, it started to fade, although the sound of those running footsteps steps grew louder.

As it passed by, there was what he described as 'the stench of death' and, as he stared after sound of the receding steps, the figure appeared once more before it vanished.

Dave Thomas was fishing alone at Brook beach one night when he was surprised to see men coming ashore in what looked like an old whaler. They were so close to the shore that he could hear their voices. One was urging the others on. "We are almost into shore, pull, pull," he said. Dave heard the sound of the boat hitting the beach and...then there was silence. The boat and its occupants had vanished. "I had my rods packed away and I was out of there," he said.

Chris Cade of Gurnard once spent many summer nights fishing at Atherfield, but he rarely went there alone after the night he heard phantom footsteps.

The spirits of smugglers and ship-wrecked sailors still walk these lonely beaches

"One night I was down on the beach and the fish were biting nicely. There was a bright moon and apart from the crashing of the waves, everything was very still. I heard footsteps coming towards me through the shingle. I shone my torch. The beach was deserted but the footsteps kept on coming. Someone or something was shuffling towards me out of the darkness."

Chris suddenly felt very frightened and reached down to grab a large stone as a weapon. Still the footsteps kept coming, and as they passed him, his nerve broke. He reeled in, grabbed some of his tackle, and with his lamp pointing towards the sound, Chris went in search of fellow angler Dick Hall.

Dick of St Mary's Road, Cowes, was taking part in the same competition that April night in 1983, and when he heard Chris's story, he understood his terror. He, too, had experienced something very strange one night while fishing alone at Chale Bay.

"It could have been between one and two o'clock when I sensed I was not alone. I knew there was something standing behind me, although the beach was empty." Addressing thin air, Dick told it, 'I don't know who you are, old mate, but you are making me nervous. I've no wish to bother you so I hope you don't mean me any harm.' At that, the unseen presence moved off down the beach towards Chale.

Neville Wheeler was fishing at a spot called 'Coastguards' one night when someone walked through the shingle towards him and placed a hand on his right shoulder. 'All right, pal,' said Neville, as he looked back to see who was behind him. He was alone.

Roger Lawrence, a long-time chairman of the Western Wight Angling Club, was night fishing at Blackgang, some distance from his friends, when he heard footsteps in the shingle, which stopped by his side.

Without looking up, Roger asked, 'anything doing down there?' There was no reply. Roger, who is convinced to this day it was not his imagination, was so unnerved by the incident that he left his tackle and would not return for it until someone agreed to go with him.

Chapter Nine

GHOSTS LIVE ON AT VENTNOR

HAUNTED OPERATING THEATRE

For almost a century, the Royal National Hospital was at the forefront of the fight against the highly infectious disease, tuberculosis.

More than 100,000 patients were treated there. Many were cured. Others weren't so fortunate. Much pioneering and experimental surgery was carried out in the operating theatre, but until the discovery of new and effective drugs, consumption was a highly infectious killer disease.

When the last patient left in May 1964, the hospital doors were locked. Five years later, the eleven blocks of balconied cottages, which stretched for almost half-a-mile, were demolished, and like a phoenix from the ashes, the Ventnor Botanic Gardens rose from the ruins.

But the old hospital did not give in gracefully. Its death throes brought ghost hunters and psychic investigators from all over the world. The hospital was haunted. Psychic activity was centred very strongly around the old operating theatre. Virtually the last part of the building to be torn down, it resisted all efforts at demolition by mechanical means. Four tractors, excavators and a ball crane were wrecked in the attempt. The operating theatre was left standing while the rest of the hospital was reduced to rubble.

Roy Dore, of St Lawrence, was curator at the time of the demolition in 1969, and worked for the former Ventnor Urban District Council which bought the 33-acre site from the Ministry of Health. He recalls what a headache the operating theatre caused for Gosport demolition contractors, Treloar and Sons. "They tried to knock it down with a crane and ball, but the steel cable snapped. Then they brought in a large tracked tractor. Three huge pieces of masonry fell on it, crushing the cab, smashing the transmission and breaking the steel tracks.

"A small caterpillar tractor with a steel hawser was used to pull the walls down, but the hook and cable attachment on the back snapped right off. Another caterpillar tractor became entangled with the broken cable from the first attempt, and at that point, they gave up."

Long after the rest of the hospital was just a pile of bricks, the empty operating theatre held out. Ether could still be smelled and Roy was among those who noticed it. Workmen talked openly of ghosts. Two men told to demolish the operating theatre with sledgehammers, were confronted by a ghost standing in a doorway.

Moaning, Weeping and Groaning

A young ghost girl looking very pale and ill, with deep sunken eyes, often appeared to keep watch on workmen as they dismantled the old hospital. John Slade of Cowes remembers her well.

Then a lad of 16, he did demolition and salvage work at the site. It was a job he will never forget. Workmen do not frighten easily, but those men at Ventnor Hospital always left the site well before darkness fell. Nearby, residents complained constantly - not about the noise and dust from the demolition - but about the moaning, weeping and groaning coming from the empty hospital buildings at night.

Grey misty shapes were seen flitting about the ruins like wisps of cloud, and the temperature around the old operating theatre always felt several degrees colder than the rest of the site. After the theatre had defied all efforts at demolition by mechanical means, John was one of those sent in with sledgehammers to finish the job by hand. "I always felt there was something very wrong there. It was like we were being watched all the time. You could be running with sweat but still feel icy cold. It was a bad place and even after it was pulled down and levelled, nothing would grow there, no weeds, no grass, and it still felt cold.

"That operating theatre was the coldest place I have ever worked in.

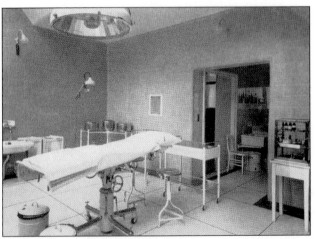

It was also the hardest to knock down. I don't know why, for it was built the same as the rest. It just didn't seem to want to go." John often saw the ghost girl standing in the corner of a ward adjoining that old theatre. She was about ten years

The operating theatre is pictured here in the 1930s

The Royal National Hospital at Ventnor was almost half a mile long

old and four feet tall. Her face and features were solid; the rest of her misty. She would appear in the early mornings or late afternoons and stand there in the ruined, roofless building, staring at the workmen. Then she would vanish.

Ghost Hunters Arrive

Finally, the site was levelled and a car park built over the top. But weird things continued to happen. A surveyor peering through his theodolite, saw two Victorian nurses pass in front of the instrument!

The former hospital became a magnet for ghost hunters and students of the supernatural who came from all over the world to try to discover its secret. News of the hauntings even reached American comedian Dick Van Dyke, who was so intrigued by the stories that he had several transatlantic telephone talks with Roy Dore about the happenings there, and featured them on his popular TV talk show in the States.

Despite a service of exorcism by local clergy, ghosts continued to make their presence felt. A four-inch thick, armour-plated power cable buried in a trench running across the operating theatre site suddenly stopped functioning, cutting off power to the Garden Tavern. When the trench was opened up, electricity board workers found the thick cable had been neatly chopped into 2ft 6in lengths. How it was done and by whom was never discovered. Meanwhile, one of the engineers replacing the cable suffered a nasty shock - but not from any electrical source.

While using the nearby toilets, situated in a block converted from the hospital shop, he glanced up to see a ghost sitting on top of the toilet door, watching him. "He came flying out of there with his trousers undone, jumped into his van and left. He never came back," recalled Roy with a grin.

With the car park surfaced over, few visitors now realise there was ever a hospital on the site. But that old operating theatre still exerts a malign and disturbing influence. Some dogs grow agitated refusing to walk across that area of the car park, and an unusually high number of accidents happen there. "If a kiddie falls down and cuts a knee, or someone trips and sprains an ankle, it will always be in that area," said Roy. "It's uncanny."

MILLY MEETS A GHOST

From the moment Milly Pugsley saw the old Royal National Hospital, she loved the place. As a student nurse, she spent two happy years there, despite several encounters with the hospital's ghosts. Now a retired nurse tutor, Milly lives in Newport, with a collection of elderly cats which she claims moved in when she wasn't looking.

When she started training in September 1952, Milly knew nothing of the hospital's dark reputation, but was introduced to one of the spirits on the top floor during her very first spell of night duty.

"It was my job to set out the cups and saucers on a tray for the patients' early morning tea. Having done that, I went downstairs to sit in the kitchen with the other nurses. Suddenly, there was a loud rattling noise as if someone was moving china about. I asked if it was mice. I was told, 'No, it's only the ghost.' This happened every night. We just accepted it and replaced all the cups and saucers before the tea round."

While on night duty in another ward, Milly was allowed two hours' sleep and given a bed in the anaesthetic room adjoining the operating theatre. "I was warned to watch out for the ghost there, so taking no chances I always made sure Orlando, a huge ginger tomcat belonging to one of the doctors, came along with me. I figured that if there were any ghosts around, Orlando would see them first," laughed Milly.

Other nurses had told her the ghost liked to pull the bedclothes up around the neck of anyone sleeping in that room, so she didn't get into bed, but lay on top, with Orlando purring beside her.

One night, Milly woke suddenly with a feeling that something was wrong. The room was silent; all the usual hospital sounds were missing. "Orlando was standing at the foot of the bed, staring into the corner of

Ventnor Botanic Gardens now occupy the site of the old hospital

the room, his fur on end. The room was normally well lit but now it was in shadow; a black shape was trying to materialise. I didn't wait to see any more. The feeling of menace in that room was awful."

Gathering her shoes, cap and the cat, Milly burst out of the room, running along the verandah to the office. The Sister on duty took one look at the terrified girl and said, "I know what's happened to you, my dear! I'll get you a nice cup of tea."

After this experience, Milly heard that the dark shadow had been seen by other staff, who said it was the ghost of an anaesthetist who had committing suicide after killing a patient by mistake.

Other incidents happened in wards near the operating theatre. Bells summoned nurses to empty rooms, and a ghostly hand set off a patient's alarm when he was unable to breathe, bringing help to him just in time.

HAND ON THE BEDCLOTHES

Some patients also saw whatever walked those hospital wards. In 1957, Violet Newman from London actually came face to face with one of the ghosts. One night as she lay in her bed facing the verandah, Violet saw the french doors swing open and a girl stepped into the room. She called out a greeting, thinking it was a fellow patient. Suddenly, one of the hospital cats which had been snoozing in the room with her, shot off down the corridor, its tail and fur standing on end. And when Violet glanced back, she was alone. The girl had vanished.

On another occasion, she was woken from a deep sleep to feel her bedclothes being rolled down, although the room was empty. "It was the nights that were the worst. Strange things happened then," said Violet.

AND STILL IT GOES ON...

Simon Goodenough doesn't believe in ghosts. A sceptic of the supernatural, he was sure the tales of hauntings at the old hospital were just ridiculous...until he met the ghost of a long-dead patient.

With a scientific background and 12 years at Kew Gardens behind him, Simon took over as curator at Ventnor Botanic Gardens in 1985. With Deb, his wife, who is also an expert in horticulture, and a staff of gardeners and workmen, Simon has transformed the former hospital gardens into a renowned centre of botanic excellence.

After just two weeks at Ventnor, Simon and Deb began to experience things they couldn't explain - silly little things - but puzzling all the same. The couple went into the new temperate house to check their plants and found both doors had been locked behind them - although the only set of keys was in Simon's pocket.

Did a ghostly hand lock Simon and Deb Goodenough in the temperate house?

The potting shed was formerly used as an 'open-air' ward for tuberculosis patients

The wooden open-air hospital wards where patients 'enjoyed' the bracing sea breezes, winter and summer, were converted into potting sheds. Here, seeds, cuttings, young plants and the gardens' index file system were kept. On several mornings, Simon arrived to find that the index cards had been removed from their files, neatly sorted, and stacked into piles on the potting bench. The doors were always still locked and padlocked. There was no sign of a break-in; just neat little piles of white cards sorted by a hand that is no longer living. "Whatever is here seemed curious about our work. The feeling we got was benign. It seemed to approve of what we are doing," said Simon.

A Sickly Ghost

For several years running, in the week before Christmas, Simon and Deb were puzzled by the smell of hot cinnamon punch, which wafted around them as they worked in the potting shed. "We both noticed it but could never find out where it was coming from," said Simon.

The mystery was solved after a chance remark to Dr Eric Laidlaw, a former doctor at the old RNH, who recalled it was hospital tradition to serve hot punch at Christmas. Huge steaming bowls were taken round on a trolley to all the patients - including those in the open-air wards.

That kindly potting shed ghost may even have saved Deb's life on the night of the great hurricane in October 1987. As she worked there alone, unaware of the impending storm, she felt an overwhelming urge to leave. It was as if someone was telling her to drop everything and get out immediately. Deb was so unnerved that she obeyed her premonition and went home.

Later that night, the potting shed was crushed when a huge tree fell on top of it. Surveying the damage the next morning, Deb said a heartfelt thanks to whoever had warned her.

One evening soon after starting his job at Ventnor, Simon met the sickly ghost of a patient from the old hospital near the potting shed. "We chatted a while. He asked if I been there long. I said about three months."

The man aged in his forties, who appeared very drawn and pale, told Simon, "I have been in the hospital now for six months." He then said 'cheerio', and wandered off.

"What he had said suddenly hit me and as I drove out of the car park, all the hairs on the back of my neck stood on end. I had just seen a ghost." Then Simon's natural scepticism took over. He told himself the man had come from a nursing home nearby.

However, two years later, he saw the figure again. This time, the apparition did not speak, but vanished as Simon watched. Wearing the same clothes as before, a heavy, old-fashioned Edwardian flannel suit, the ghostly patient still looked very ill.

"I was sure then that I had been speaking to a ghost...a very sickly and consumptive one who must have died here at Ventnor."

After more than 25 years as curator, Simon has left Ventnor Botanic Gardens for new horticultural challenges. The ghosts however, remain.

(Read more tales from the haunted hospital in *Isle of Wight Ghosts Book Four, Ghost Island* and *Even More Ghosts*)

Chapter Ten

KNIGHTON GORGES - THAT MOST HAUNTED HOUSE

It has been called the most haunted place on the Island, and even today, the long-vanished house of Knighton Gorges seems determined to live up to its reputation. Strange things happen there still, and according to some, what was once described as the most beautiful of the Island's ancient manors, can still be seen at midnight on New Year's Eve. (The haunting history of the house is told in *The Original Ghosts of the Isle of Wight*)

Describing Knighton Gorges in her book 'A Cavalier's Ladye' Constance MacEwen wrote, *'Nothing but a fine gateway, surmounted by the mutilated arms of the Dillingtons, and a walled kitchen garden, with an ancient stone arbour built in, remains to indicate the approach to the mansion, except two large basins of water, which were ornamental lakes in the days when Sir Tristram Dillington, mounted on his favourite charger Thunderbolt, rode furiously down Knighton Shute and through the gates, up the long avenue still indicated by a few remaining trees.*

Sir Tristram was undoubtedly one of Knighton Gorges' most colourful owners. He was MP for Newport, a Major in the Guards, and a breeder of fine horses. One story handed down by Newchurch folk has him married with four children to carry on the Dillington line. But in 1721, according to legend, his entire family contracted a fever. Within a fortnight, his wife and children were dead. Sir Tristram, frantic with grief, killed himself.

The probable truth is rather less romantic. Sir Tristram, at 43, had neither wife nor children. A bachelor with two spinster sisters Mary and Hannah, he lived a lonely life at Knighton Gorges. He was a reckless gambler and subject to fits of depression. Whether he drowned himself in a lake on the estate or shot himself, is unclear. Whichever method he chose, as a suicide his property should have gone to the Crown. But on discovering the body, his good and faithful steward turned his master's favourite horse, Thunderbolt, loose with a broken girth and spread the story of a riding accident. The estate was saved. The grateful sisters rewarded him with a farm.

However he met his end, Sir Tristram has slept fitfully since. It was not long after his death on July 4th 1721, that local folk began to avoid

Knighton Gorges is pictured here in 1816, just five years before it was totally demolished

Knighton Shute after dark. A spectral hound was seen, followed by a headless horseman. From a sealed room in the old house came an agony of wailing. Through succeeding centuries, there have been numerous reports of Sir Tristram's ghost driving a coach and four on the anniversary of his death.

Since he was a boy, Knighton Gorges has held a strange fascination for Ivor Davies, a retired consultant engineer and former Mayor of South Wight Borough Council. Ivor fulfilled a childhood dream when he bought six acres of land on which the old house once stood, where he has converted a 17th century stone barn into a holiday cottage.

Ivor has spent years researching the history of Knighton Gorges, and although he has never seen or heard a ghost there, he is quite prepared to believe that others have. "So many people have told me of their experiences that I am quite disappointed nothing has yet happened for me," said Ivor, who recalls cycling out to Knighton Gorges as a boy to play there with friends. "People are drawn to the place but I understand the strange attraction that brings them."

With the help of old documents, records and engravings, Ivor has been able to trace the outlines of the house. He has found the remains of the foundations and part of the gardens and has researched its owners back to the Middle Ages. Ivor has his own ideas on its demolition.

Legend tells that it was done out of spite by Captain Maurice George Bisset when his eldest daughter married against his wishes. The bitter old man died, it was said, in a tiny gardener's cottage in the grounds, breathing his last as the timbers and stones crashed down on December 16th 1821.

Ivor holds a less romantic but far more practical theory. He believes the upkeep of the old house was simply too great. It had fallen into disrepair; it was costing too much to maintain and Captain Bisset had it demolished and sold off everything he could. Evidence to support this theory survives nearby.

The back staircase from Knighton Gorges, once used by servants, is now in Horringford House in Arreton, (pictured on page 88) while part of the main staircase is at nearby Langbridge House, Newchurch. Stone and timber from the old manor was used in other houses built in the 1820s, including Veniscombe House in Newchurch (see chapter eight).

Whatever the reason for its demolition, Bisset undoubtedly died along with his house. However, parts of the ancient manor of Knighton Gorges do still exist ...

A GHOST ON THE STAIRS

Today the gleaming, polished wooden staircase, which once graced the splendid hall in Knighton Gorges, is less than a mile from the long-gone manor house. Local nobility and distinguished visitors such as John Wilkes, David Garrick and Sir Joshua Reynolds once walked upon its boards.

The staircase, or at least part of it, has been incorporated into nearby Langbridge House, Newchurch, and with it has gone one of the manor's ancient ghosts. The stooped and hooded figure of an elderly friar was seen by Ivy Welstead during a meeting of the local Women's Institute at the old house.

Ivy recalled, "The spirit appeared to be aged about seventy; he was not solid but transparent and grey. He looked a very benevolent old gentleman and I was not at all frightened. He stood at the top of the staircase, and then just disappeared into a wall."

This staircase is now at Langbridge House

Ivy decided to keep this sighting to herself in case her fellow WI members were alarmed, but she later told Jill Salmon and her husband Frank, owners of Langbridge since 1968, about her experience. Neither Frank, a former airline pilot, nor ex-air stewardess Jill, saw their ghost, and apart from one or two 'odd' accidents on the staircase, they said they had always been happy there.

Did the grey friar accompany the old staircase to Langbridge House? It seems likely, for Parson James Tooke purchased an assortment of materials from Knighton Gorges after it was demolished. Distinctively carved doors and door frames, beams, tiles and stonework from the old mansion live on in Langbridge House.

Built in 1725 on the site of an old farmhouse, Langbridge House stands opposite the Old School House Cottage (whose ghostly history features in chapter seven). Parson Tooke's bargain buys from Knighton Gorges, which was pulled down in 1821, were later incorporated into Langbridge House when it was remodelled.

But the vicar clearly got more than he bargained for when he purchased that old staircase. Does the weary spirit of an elderly friar, which once haunted the manor house, live on in those vestiges of its former glory?

This staircase is at Horringford House

GHOSTLY GREEN WINDOWS

As midnight approached on New Year's Eve 1991, Brian Perkins, his wife Lois, and two friends, decided to drive out to Knighton Gorges to see if any of the stories about the old house re-appearing on that night were true.

Taking their Doberman bitch, Anya, along with them, they drove out to Knighton where they were amazed to find many others with the same idea. Brian, of Partlands Avenue, Ryde, said it was a cold clear night with good visibility. "We walked through the gateposts into the grounds. Just after midnight, we saw the outline of a stone window appear in the distance. It was glowing and a luminous green colour."

The apparition lasted for almost a minute and during this time he and the others ran towards it, even climbing a barbed wire fence to get closer. The window faded, re-appeared, and then faded away again. All four agreed it had been a large, square, ground floor stone window. As they returned to the van, Brian heard the sound of a horse and carriage clattering through the gates of Knighton Gorges. He could see nothing but the phantom folds of a blue cloak high above the ground - where a spectral coachman had been sitting.

Meanwhile, back in their van, the dog, which was usually very quiet, was agitated, refusing to calm down until they had put Knighton Gorges and its haunting atmosphere far behind them.

"We were all astonished by what we had seen. We had not gone expecting anything to happen. It was all supposed to be a bit of a laugh. But I certainly believe there is something there now," said Brian.

BATHED IN AN EERIE LIGHT

One autumn evening in 1969, Ray Harvey and a girlfriend were sitting in his car in a lay-by on the Downs road, listening to the radio and looking out over Sandown Bay. The evening was dark and still.

Suddenly, the countryside grew as bright as day; for perhaps two or three seconds, daylight appeared over Knighton Gorges. "There was no sound; it was no lightning flash; simply a brief period of daylight on what had been a lovely dark September night. It was like an eclipse in reverse. We both saw it, but to this day, I have absolutely no idea what it was," said Ray. He was amazed to find nothing on the local news to explain the strange event, and more surprised that no one else had seen it. For those brief moments, everything in the area of Knighton Gorges was bathed in light. Was it perhaps the old house making one of its rare appearances? From where he was sitting, Ray couldn't see.

Although she was not the girlfriend involved, Ray's wife Mandy certainly didn't scoff at this tale, for she too saw something strange and disturbing at Knighton Gorges.

RIDDLE OF THE STONE CREATURES

Mandy, a former nurse, is one of the few people who have seen the stone lions atop the old gateposts at Knighton Gorges. As a teenager, she frequently passed the pillars while out horse riding and was attracted to the beasts, which she described as "large crouching lions with their paws in front, carved out of old weathered grey stone."

Years later when she worked in Newchurch, Mandy regularly drove past the old gateposts. One day she noticed the stone beasts were gone. When she mentioned it at work and asked what had happened to them, everyone laughed. There had been nothing on those gateposts in living memory, they told her.

A REAL MYSTERY TOUR

Countless times in the 1950s and early '60s, local coach driver Ted Perry took visitors on mystery tours down Knighton Shute and through Newchurch. He always stopped by the gateposts to tell his passengers the story of Knighton Gorges, of how the old house had been demolished and only the gateposts, with their heraldic lions on top, had been spared.

Ted, who lived at a little cottage in Brading Mall, has now sadly died. However, it was a letter he wrote to the Isle of Wight County Press in 1965 that first posed the riddle of the stone creatures which has intrigued Islanders ever since.

Ted had taken his passengers past the gateposts and stopped as usual to tell them the Knighton Gorges story. But to his amazement, when he looked at the pillars, the animals had disappeared. Fearing they had been stolen, he dashed off an angry letter to the newspaper asking if anyone knew where they were. For a long while after this, controversy raged.

A number of Islanders claimed to have seen the creatures despite photographs dating from 1916 and 1949 which provided clear evidence

There are no stone creatures here. This photograph taken in 1949 shows only the gateposts with their ornamental stone 'loaves of bread' sitting on top

that the only ornamentation in recent years had been the circular hoops known locally as 'loaves of bread', a traditional sign to hungry travellers that they would be given bread and water at the kitchen door to speed them on their way.

Ted finally accepted the creatures weren't there - although he had been pointing them out to his passengers for years. "None of them ever said a word. They must have thought I was mad, or they all saw the figures themselvelves," he laughed.

PHANTOM IN A BALL GOWN

Knighton Gorges continues to draw people. Its reputation as the Island's most haunted place is well known, and every New Year's Eve hopeful ghost hunters converge there, hoping for a glimpse of the old house, which is said to materialise on that night.

Among the watchers on December 31st 1982 was Judy Axford, who

The Island's most haunted place - this is all that remains of the ancient manor house of Knighton Gorges - a stone kitchen wall hidden amongst the pines

went there with a friend. As the two women stood on the drive by the old stone gateposts, Judy who has psychic abilities, became aware of a woman in a long mauve dress moving towards them at speed.

"The figure came from the left of the gateposts. It was moving very quickly and I could not see its feet or legs. It was a young woman with fair hair piled high on top of her head. She was wearing a very decorative ball gown. It was the colour of the gown that first caught my attention. It was absolutely gorgeous," Judy added.

Suddenly she felt icy cold, and with her friend, who had also seen the figure, Judy got back into her car and drove off up Knighton Shute before her passenger had even closed her door.

They returned to Newchurch and parked outside the 900-year-old church at the top of Newchurch Shute. "We sat quietly, looking out over the village towards Knighton Gorges, hoping we might see the house - but from a safe distance."

But they saw nothing at all. Newchurch slumbered through the old year and into the new. But Judy did hear something; it was the sound of a whip cracking. A ghostly echo, perhaps, of a phantom carriage carrying revellers from that ball where the mauve lady had been a guest.

Few pictures of Knighton Gorges remain today. This engraving from Worsley's History of the Isle of Wight shows the north-western side of the old house

DOOM AND BLACKNESS

In a strange postscript to this narrative of Knighton Gorges, an Island hotelier and Newport businessman, the late Malcolm Calvert, once owned what was believed to be Captain Bisset's watch. A heavy silver, steel-faced pocket watch, it was contained in a silver case with a convex glass. Made by Hunt of London, in the back of the case was a piece of faded red silk bearing the captain's name written with the old-fashioned long 's'.

The watch was examined by a local psychic, who was told *nothing* of the watch's ownership or of its connection with Knighton Gorges. Presumably, Maurice George Bisset knew the sad story of Sir Tristram Dillington and his suicide. For in addition to comments about Bisset himself, she was aware of the older events, which had occurred in the manor he had destroyed.

Holding the watch she said, "I see someone riding with a heavy heart. There seems to be an accident or suicide. Perhaps it was arranged to say one thing when it was the other because it looked better. I see water. I see a man in the water.

People decide to change the facts. They twist the facts..."

Apart from this remarkably accurate picture of Sir Tristram's death, she gave descriptions of people and places which fit the known facts of the notorious Worsley-Bisset trial and its background.

She spoke of a tall impressive building with guests arriving in fine carriages; of gaming at which large sums changed hands; of intrigue and deception; of much travel between the Island and the mainland and of two men and a 'lovely coquettish woman'.

One of the men, she said, came to an unhappy end. Vividly she described a sick man with a gaunt face lying in a carved and curtained bed, which looked out of place in the poor bare room that contained it. (Captain Bisset was said to have died in his gardener's cottage).

And still in a trance she added, "There was a passion which burned with vengeance, a passion which was destructive. The ill effects are still going on... doom and blackness."

Is the malignant passion of Maurice George Bisset so strong that it lives on, where a ruined gateway leads to a haunted hill at the place that still bears the name of Knighton Gorges?

THE END